FOREX
SIMPLIFIED

Behind the Scenes of Currency Trading

FOREX
SIMPLIFIED
Behind the Scenes of Currency Trading

MARILYN MCDONALD

Marketplace Books
Glenelg, Maryland

ISBN: 1-59280-316-4

ISBN 13: 978-1-59280-316-3

Even a thousand-mile journey begins with a first step.

I would like to thank my extremely supportive partner and husband, Patrick Nouvion, without him, this book would never have been written. I would also like to thank my parents for raising me to believe I can be or do whatever I like; my angelic son for understanding all the times mom was working and unable to check out his latest video game level; Todd Crosland for believing in me and giving me the opportunity to grow; and countless others for helping me along my path.

Table of Contents

PREFACE

Let me introduce myself. My name is Marilyn and I am a currency trader. Not only am I a trader, but I have been working in the trading industry for a number of years. I am a Series 3 Licensed Futures Broker, currently working for a Forex brokerage, and I have also spent a number of years working for a company that produces and sells technical analysis software. The point of this is not to impress you, not at all. The point is that I have been exposed to the theories and heard the sales pitches; heck, I have even given some of them (not proud of that, by the way). I have also seen what and who lies behind some of those theories and pitches.

I like to equate my experience to the city of Las Vegas. It is shiny and beautiful, and everything sparkles. However, give it a little time and you start to notice the cracks in the façade. You notice that the sequins may be a little cheap and tattered, and everything isn't really as it seems. In reality, the entire place is set up to do one thing—take your money. Don't get me wrong, the buildings are beautiful; but, if you just look at the outside, you can get the wrong picture if you are not careful.

The best example of this is the predominant myth that trading is easy. So many people get into the trading game, and specifically the Forex market, because they think it is easy. They believe that this will be the way they can make their fortune and retire. I am sure you have heard the claims of ordinary people who have made their fortune in mere weeks or months. How about losses? In fact, the *Wall Street Journal* recently quoted the CEO of a leading Forex brokerage as saying, "If 15% of the Forex traders were successful, I would be surprised."

The reality is that trading, especially Forex, takes discipline. It takes a certain level of commitment and it involves risk. Lots of risk.

The reason I wrote this book is not to frighten you away from the currency trading realm. It is simply to give you a behind the scenes look at what happens here. I want to tell you what other people don't. I am not going to sell you my fabulous system. I will not tell you what and when to trade. If this is what you are after, then please put this book down and pick up another. There are plenty of others who will sell you what you want to hear. When you are sick of the gloss and sales pitches, then come back and take a walk with me, behind the scenes in the currency market.

Introduction

If I held a mirror to the individual investors in the current foreign exchange trading market, the reflection would be a growing gamut of Forex traders with diverse demographics. This is because the Forex market is the largest financial market in the world with over $1.9 trillion in foreign currencies changing hands every day. Considering this depth and breadth, you might expect the Forex trader population to be a melting pot of people from a variety of backgrounds.

Here in the United States, this lucrative market was traditionally reserved for the large banks and the big boys. Individual U. S. citizens were not able to trade foreign currencies before 1999; but, with the change in federal law and regulation by the Commodities Futures Trading Commission (CFTC) in 2000, all of this began to change.

U.S. traders have discovered what Asian and European traders have known for a long time—the average person can do well trading Forex. Forex is entering more and more home offices, small independent money management firms and the lives of men and women every day. In fact, currency trading by individuals in the United States is growing by about 50 percent per year.

Widespread availability of high-speed Internet access is another factor that has leveled the playing field between the establishment and the small traders. Today, it is easy to download and install a trading platform that provides access to real-time currency prices, a demo or test account to begin and train with, and charting and technical analysis assistance. This means that traders from varied walks of life can participate. And it doesn't require a small fortune to get started. In fact, you can find everything you need for free on the Internet.

My friend and fellow trader, Ed Ponsi, who is also president of FX Educator, says Forex trading is for "anyone and everyone." Ed, who is also a money manager and consultant, continues, "Trading is so democratic now. Anyone can learn how to trade with the opportunities that are available today. There is so much money out there now, with the huge influx of capital into hedge funds, that anyone with a good track record and the right mental attitude can get a piece of the action."

It is with that brand of encouragement from Forex advocates like Ed Ponsi that even novice traders are diversifying their portfolios by entering the Forex market. Male and female, single or married, work-at-home moms, 43-year-old males with over 20 years of trading experience, they are all taking the initiative to trade Forex.

The firm I work for, **Interbank FX**, is seeing men and women, old and young, from all over the world become Forex traders. We have customers in over 135 countries and are opening over 40,000 demo accounts every month. All of our business is done over the Internet; and, on the Internet no one knows that you are not a member of the old guard.

Some of our customers are women who supplement their household income by making small trades a few hours a week. I also know of college students and recent graduates who have jumped into Forex because it offered them an opportunity to expand their already independent, technology savvy lifestyle with a small, startup fund.

"I think today's trader is a tech-savvy, independent thinker, the kind of person who takes the initiative," says Ponsi. "Traders have always been an independent breed, with little patience for the constrictions of the nine-to-five job. Today's technology gives them the means to raise the level of their knowledge as high as they desire, without limits."

Another fellow Forex trader, 25-year-old Chris Murdock, who has been trading for three years, sees that "the potential is certainly there" for people of his age to invest in Forex. "I think people are being exposed to a form of investment that was not readily available until fairly recently." Murdock continues, "It seems that previously only people that had a large amount of capital could invest in the Forex market. It's getting away from the pressed suit, tie-wearing business types. It's moving to more 'normal' people. The guy working in the car garage, working the cash register at the grocery store, or even your taxi driver could be a Forex trader."

The Forex market will continue to grow, not just with the world's economies of currency, but with the diversity of traders it has already shown it possesses.

FOREX
SIMPLIFIED
Behind the Scenes of Currency Trading

Chapter One:
Why Choose Forex?

Of all the markets I have checked out and could have started my trading debut with, why did I choose the Forex market? Well, that is a valid question. The Forex market has some very attractive properties, but first some history. The traditional Forex market participants are large central banks, Interbank brokers, hedge funds, and commercial companies. These are not your everyday banks and brokers; these are the big sharks. It has been said that the Chinese central banks intervene in the Forex market to the tune of $1 billion every day. So you, as a retail Forex trader, are the smallest fish in this gigantic ocean.

It is not uncommon for a large bank to trade billions on a daily basis. Most of this activity is conducted by the trading desks, where dealers trade to make the bank profits. National central banks also play a critical role in the Forex market. These central banks try to control money supply and sometimes have target rates for their currencies. Many of these central banks have substantial foreign exchange reserves, which makes their intervention power significant. One of the roles of a central bank is in the restoration of an orderly market in times of excessive exchange rate volatility. They also aid in the control of the inflationary impact of a weakening currency. However, central banks are not all powerful; if the market participants really want to take on a central bank, the combined resources of the market can overwhelm the banks influence. Remember, no one party can control the Forex market, not for long.

Hedge fund traders have emerged as aggressive currency speculators in recent years. With the rate at which these funds have been increasing, the size and liquidity of the Forex market can be very appealing.

Protection against unfavorable market moves is one of the primary reasons why this market is even in existence, and commercial companies have been part of the backbone of the Forex markets. Although many companies trade in sizes that are insignificant to short-term market moves, one of the factors that determines the long-term direction of a currency's exchange rate is the overall trade flow.

Enter the Everyday Trader

Speculators (that's you and me) play an increasingly important role in the market, taking over the risks that commercial participants don't wish to be exposed to. So with more traders entering the markets each month, it is interesting to look at why Forex trading is so popular. The following paragraphs will help answer that question.

Diversification

You know the old adage about putting your eggs in one basket, right? The long and the short of it is that you shouldn't. Like many other Americans, I have a 401k, a bit of real estate, a little bit in a managed fund, a checking account or two, and a money market account. The bulk of my assets were based on the U.S. dollar and economy. That is not necessarily a good thing.

Let's take a look at a worst-case scenario. If Utah had a catastrophic event, then my property values would probably tank. I have insurance, but I get the feeling that one doesn't really know the extent of coverage until one actually needs the coverage, so I may or may not get the insurance money for what I feel is the worth of my property. Let's go one step further and add insult to injury and suppose that the U.S. stock market hits a reversal and my other assets start to take a slide. This is a potentially rough way to find out that my portfolio isn't as diversified as I had planned. In light of these possibilities, I decided that the Forex market was attractive as a way to diversify my meager portfolio.

One of the benefits of trading currency is that I could very easily invest in another countries' currency without doing the twelve-hour drive north to Canada to open a bank account to store my "Loonies" in. With the click of one or two buttons, I could place my confidence in the Euro, the Yen, or a number of other currencies from around the world. Now, if the worst-case scenario hits and the stock market takes a little slide, there is a possibility that I can make a gain on other currencies.

24 Hour Trading

It is hard to day trade stocks without giving up your day job, and that certainly wasn't an option for me. Like many others, I usually scramble home from a long day at work, fix and eat dinner, hang out with the kid, and peer at my charts a little before shuffling off to bed. Trading in a market with fixed hours seemed impossible for me. If there did happen to be a good trade on the horizon, I would have had to squeeze placing orders into the morning rush of snoozing the alarm, rushing to get ready, and bolting down that first cup of coffee. It was enough to make me throw up my hands and reach for the nearest money manager.

As a contrast, the Forex market is open 24 hours a day, 5 1/2 days a week. This means my two hours of chart watching in the evenings can be accompanied by actual trading. In fact, I have heard from numerous traders that the best time to trade is the middle of the night. I am not sure how this works since I have heard it from people in Australia, England, and in all US time zones. I have found that no matter what the time zone, there always are trading opportunities that are making the Forex market particularly convenient for people like me who are living life as well as trading.

Volatility

One of the other things that interested me about the Forex market is the volatility. There isn't another market out there that exhibits the schizophrenic behavior that the currency market does. This means that the hour or two I spend trading every evening can bring about some lucrative results. Remember though that the risk and potential for loss are equally as possible, but we will come back to that shortly.

Liquidity

The likelihood of being able to get into and out of trades at any given time during the day or night is very high in the Forex market. There are literally hundreds of thousands of people online every second during the market hours buying and selling currencies. The market itself trades approximately $1.9 trillion every single day.

Low Fees

Actually, there aren't really fees when you trade Forex. The trader's cost of doing business is called the spread. That is essentially the difference between the price you can buy the currency and the price you can sell the currency (the "bid" and the "ask"). For example, if you have a bid price on the EUR USD of 1.2733 and an ask price of 1.2735, you are "paying" a two pip spread. There are no other commissions or hidden fees. If there are, do a Google search for Forex brokers because you may have the wrong one.

It works a little like this: if I placed a buy on the EUR USD at 1.2733, I won't see a break even on the trade until the price moves to 1.2735. So if I were trading a mini account, I would see a -$2 on that particular trade. (My account is held in USD; if I had an account in some other currency that value might be a little different.) Once the price moves to 1.2735, my profit comes out of the red and heads for the green.

Ease

Let's face it, getting started in Forex trading is easy, sometimes too easy, but we will get back to that. The barriers to entry are low and in most instances, you can open an account online in a matter of a day or two. Then you pop a check in the mail, and you are ready to hit the big time. Most Forex brokers will let you open a mini account for as little as $250, and because of the leverage inherent in this industry, you can be off and trading large amounts of money in no time.

Increased Leverage

Leverage is sort of like a promissory note from your broker. In its basic form, it enables a trader with 200:1 leverage to have $50 in margin controlling a $10,000 position in the market, or a 0.5% of the position value. The substantial leverage that is available to online Forex traders can be a powerful money making tool. The need for so much leverage is due to the price stability and liquidity associated with the market. These factors result in an average daily percentage movement of about 1% on major currencies, compared to the volatility of the equities markets that can easily have movements of 10% a day.

No One Person or Economy Can Control the Market

There is no physical central exchange for the Forex market. In fact, the Forex market is so vast and has so many participants that no single entity, not even a central bank, can control the market price for an extended period of time. Even interventions by mighty central banks are becoming increasingly ineffectual and short lived.

These are just some of the many reasons that I chose to trade the Forex. These are reasons that may or may not be attractive to you. The Forex market is an exciting and energetic place to trade, and it can be quite lucrative if you are prepared to be disciplined, or if you are extremely lucky.

Chapter Two:
What You Need to Know About Forex Trading

I have been around this game for awhile and have seen novice traders work themselves into an absolute lather over things that shouldn't faze them. They are usually fairly minor traps or bits of information but; if, you don't know, then you could be taken by surprise and suffer an unfortunate blood pressure spike.

Swap—What Is It and Why Does it Matter?

Forex positions that are open at the end of the business day are rolled over to the new date. As part of the rollover, positions are subject to a charge or credit based on the interest rates of the two currencies with an added markup of +/- 0.25 – 0.75%. This is referred to as swap. If you bought a currency with a higher interest rate than the one you sold, you would have a positive amount credited into your account as part of the daily rollover.

Most brokers publish their swap rates on their websites or in their platforms. However, if you want to calculate the swap yourself, the formula is:

Swap rate (short % or long %) × pip value
x number of lots x number of days

Remember that for some pairs the pip values are fixed and for others it fluctuates. Additionally, the date used in the calculation is always two bank days later. It works like this: if you open your trade on a Monday and keep it until Tuesday, it counts as if you opened it on a Wednesday and kept it until Thursday. However, if you opened the position on Wednesday and keep it until Thursday, it counts as if you opened it on Friday and kept it until Monday. That is why triple swaps apply to all positions that are held on Wednesdays. Swap is usually converted to your base currency at the time of calculation.

It is interesting to note that there are a number of trading strategies that center around hedging their trades and earning swap.

There are also certain religions that forbid the paying or receiving of interest payments. Most brokerages will offer swap free accounts to these people. These accounts usually have a commission or a fee assessed to each trade. Be prepared to prove your case here. There have been a number of abuses and brokers are rightfully suspicious of people asking for swap accounts. They will also be monitoring your trades to make sure you are placing trades on each side of the interest rate. If you continually place trades where you have had to "pay" swap, you will raise suspicion that you are earning swap at another broker and hedging with a swap free account. This practice is heavily frowned upon and you could have your trading rights suspended.

Be Aware of Fraudulent Schemes

According to industry analysts, the foreign exchange market is said to be growing at 22 – 25% per year, with the retail sector (individual investors) growing at a stronger pace than the industrial sector. As this market continues to grow, so do the number of less-than-reputable schemes associated with the industry. Recently, a probe into the biggest foreign exchange scam in U.S. history concluded with a $33 million dollar fine. The fine went to a man who solicited millions of dollars from unsuspecting investors to fund the purchase of 22 luxury cars, eight homes, and extravagant entertainment.

In this particular case, our less-than-reputable-party started soliciting customers in 1998 and offering off-exchange Forex options and futures contracts. In the process of doing so, this party grossly misrepresented the profits and risks involved in Forex trading. Adding insult to injury, the funds were never invested but were used to pay for personal expenses such as homes, cars, and boats. In order to avoid detection, the guilty party provided customers with false account statements and posted false information on his web site regarding the trading profits, market conditions and opportunities, the balances in each investor's account, and the reason for delays in paying customer's withdrawals.

Most less-than-reputable schemes have some telltale properties and can be identified by experienced traders; however, newer speculators may have problems spotting the difference between what is legitimate and what isn't. I would strongly recommend thoroughly researching any potential companies you may be thinking about investing with before sending in your hard earned cash. I am constantly surprised by how people will send checks off to companies that promise the moon without doing even the smallest bit of due diligence. These rational people who research their purchases thoroughly, read consumer reports, and weigh their options carefully about things such as schools, homes, even banks are still somehow blinded by the promise of easy riches. So, if you learn nothing else from this book, remember to do your due diligence on any company you may send your investment dollars to. The last thing you need is to find out that the company you have invested with is under investigation for fraud. In this type of circumstance, it can often be impossible to retrieve your money.

This leads me to the question, "How do you know if you have encountered a less-than-reputable deal?" Here are a few telltale signs that may help you spot this kind of shady deal before you invest.

Stay Away From Opportunities That Sound Too Good to Be True

Red flags must be raised when a firm guarantees large profits will be made. First of all, most regulatory bodies don't allow guarantees. They require that all companies that have registered provide balanced statements, which means any statement implying gains must be balanced by statements of risk. Over-inflated guarantees and statements of gain are merely ploys to entice investors and make them believe their money is safe and that they are likely to make huge returns. It is important to note that even the best professional traders cannot and do not guarantee they will make a profit on any given day. The Forex market is the most unpredictable of all the financial markets, so be suspicious of such claims and those who make them.

Stay Away From Companies That Promise Little or No Financial Risk

If you encounter any firm that claims to have developed a foreign currency trading strategy that carries very little or no risk, run away at top speed with your checkbook firmly in hand. The reason that Forex trading can be very profitable is because it also carries a very high risk of loss. The Forex market is very volatile, and even with good money management, an investor can lose most, if not more than an entire account in a very short period of time.

Be Sure to Get the Company's Performance Track Record

Before you give money to a Forex company, make sure you check them out. See whether they are registered with the United States Commodity Futures Trading Commission (www.cftc.gov) or the National Futures Association (www.nfa.futures.org). Many disreputable companies falsely claim that their firms are approved by the CFTC or NFA to gain a prospective investor's trust. This is a big red flag. The NFA and the CFTC will never "approve" of a company. You can be "registered with" but not "approved by." Other sources of helpful information may also include your state's securities commission, attorney general, and the Better Business Bureau.

Stay Away From Employment Ads "Wanting" Forex Traders

Many less-than-reputable schemes use employment ads to attract individuals with capital to trade using their systems. The ads, which often appear in newspapers and on the Internet, state that a foreign currency firm is looking for individuals to teach how to trade the using the firm's capital. Those who reply to the ad are typically convinced by the firm that they will make a fortune trading currencies if they participate in the firm's trading program. During the training process, which often occurs on a demo system, the novice traders are encouraged and told that their demo trading records show significant profits, that they are ready to make real money, and that they will be very successful. Despite the firm's assessment of the novice trader as a brilliant newcomer, no firm capital is provided to the trader; instead, the excited novice is told to use their own capital to trade using the firm's platform.

Stay Away From Firms That Pressure You to Trade Today

Investment scams usually use some compelling reason why it is essential for you to invest right now. Perhaps because the investment opportunity can be "offered to only a limited number of people" or because delaying the investment could mean missing out on a large profit. (After all, once the information they have confided to you becomes generally known, the price is sure to move, right?) Urgency is important to swindlers. For one thing, they want your money as quickly as possible with a minimum of effort on their part. And they don't want you to have time to think it over, discuss it with someone who might suggest you become suspicious, or check the proposal out with a regulatory agency. Besides, he may not plan on remaining in town very long. Please remember, the market will be here tomorrow, in six months and even next year.

Chapter Three:
The Majors

The four currencies that are traded the most are called the majors. The majors are generally the U.S. dollar (USD), the British pound (GBP or cable), the Japanese yen (JPY), and the Swiss franc (CHF or the swissy). The major pairs that are traded are the EUR/USD, the USD/JPY, the GBP/USD, and the USD/CHF.

The U.S. Dollar

The U.S. dollar features in many of the currency pairs that are traded worldwide. But the dollar hasn't always been the world's darling when it comes to reserve currencies, and there are fears that it might not be in the future. Forex traders are constantly exposed to doom and gloom tidings that seem to center around the U.S. dollar. What you need to consider is that despite the doomsday scenarios, U.S. currency has not collapsed and foreign banks, in particular Asian ones, continue to hold trillions in U.S. dollar reserves. I have heard estimates of up to two-thirds of all global central bank holdings are U.S. dollars, though official reserve holdings and allocations are not really published anywhere.

Global foreign reserve assets have been estimated to be rising in recent years, particularly in Asian, Russian, and Middle Eastern central banks. The reasons behind that are pretty clear:

- Chinese and Asian central banks have benefited from substantial export generated revenues, bringing in a large influx of U.S. dollars.

- American corporations have been buying Chinese businesses and manufacturing in China.

- It has been said the Chinese authorities intervene in the Forex market to the tune of $1 billion every trading day, buying U.S. dollars and selling their own currency to keep it from appreciating.

- With crude oil futures shooting up, oil rich Middle Eastern countries have been seeing large amounts of dollar assets into their coffers. It is hard to identify the extent of the reserve dollars held in the Middle East and in particular Saudi Arabia because they either channel funds into other agencies or stock up on U.S. fixed-income securities via U.K. investment houses.

The U.S. dollar has not always been the preferred reserve currency, though it may seem like it. The U.S. dollar seized the honor from the pound sterling around the end of World War II. There seems to be a pervasive fear in certain circles that China will sell off their U.S. holdings, pulling the rug out from under the U.S. dollar and sending U.S. interest rates climbing. In reality though, it is not in the best interests of China to sell off these holdings in large amounts. They would simply be devaluing their own portfolio. Plus, soaring U.S. interest rates would dampen the U.S. consumers spending and decrease the demand for the billions of dollars of Chinese manufactured products.

It is true that several central banks have diversified out of the dollar to some extent. Russian central banks have shifted some dollar assets into euros and have announced plans for additional diversification into yen. However, this move has been influenced by and patterned after their trading activity, which is centered largely in European zone countries. South Korea has been considering diversifying part of its reserves away from U.S. holdings into overseas blue chip stocks.

What Other Currencies Could Possibly Usurp the U.S. Dollar's Throne?

The factors that influence whether a currency is a good candidate for a reserve currency include the stability of the country itself, including its government, economy, military and politics. The stability of the currency is important as well as having substantial liquidity. The currency should also be used as an international medium of exchange; and, while the euro is an attractive contender, it has only really been around since 1999 and lacks a euro bond market to act as a compliment. On the flip side, its growth and stability have been cited as positive traits. Its liquidity has also been steadily increasing and adding to the euros' appeal. The British pound has also been touted as a possible replacement, and Commonwealth countries are most likely already holding a portion of their reserves in the cable. Some have even speculated that the Chinese currency could emerge as a reserve currency in the next several decades.

In reality, I think that the central banks are simply doing what all good investors are doing: diversifying. Moving portions of a federal reserve into euros, yen, and other currencies is simply about risk management and looking to deliver a return. While this doesn't necessarily mean the U.S. dollar will retain its title as the world's preferred reserve currency, it should dispel some of the doom and gloom that has been floating around the industry lately. Remember, it took years for the U.S. dollar to usurp the British pound.

The Euro

The euro was born on January 1, 1999, signaling the end of currencies such as the Deutsche mark, the French frank, and the Italian lira. Out of the 27 countries that make up the European Union, thirteen of them use the euro as their currency. Eleven countries initially joined to form the Eurozone—Austria, Belgium, Finland, France, Germany, Ireland, Italy, Luxembourg, Netherlands, Portugal, and Spain. Greece joined in 2001 and Slovenia joined in 2007. As a result the euro has surpassed the U.S. dollar as far as total value of cash in circulation.

With the inception of the euro, there has been no need for member countries to have their own central banks. The European Central Bank (ECB) sets the interest rates and creates the monetary policy for the entire Eurozone. Individual countries still track and report their own economic data, however the figures are also kept for the Eurozone in its entirety.

The Eurozone will add eleven more countries beginning in 2008 and finishing in 2014—Malta, Cyprus, Slovakia, Estonia, Lithuania, Bulgaria, Hungary, Latvia, Czech Republic, Poland, and Romania.

The Japanese Yen

The yen is the official Japanese currency and is usually denoted by a ¥ or JPY. The yen was established as the official unit of currency by the New Currency Act of 1871. This moved Japan onto the Gold Standard. The currency was named the "yen" because of the direct translation to "round object." Yen literally means circle.

Rising crude oil prices influence the Yen. Because it imports all of its oil as export-dependent nation, Japan is highly sensitive to rising energy costs. Japan's foreign trade industry maintains an isolationist view and they tend to lag behind the rest of the world with regards to foreign trade. However, the Yen is increasingly held as a reserve currency by central banks worldwide. One thing to notice is that when the strength of the yen rises, it tends to hurt the manufacturing industry of Japan, which is a large component of the Japanese economy.

Recently the term yen "carry traders" has been in the news, so I will offer a short explanation. Essentially, an individual borrows yen from a Japanese bank at a low interest rate (like 0.5%). That individual then exchanges the yen for U.S. dollars and buys U.S. Treasury Notes that yield about 4.5%. After one year, $1000 USD becomes $1045 USD. The theory is that after interest expenses on the 0.5%, our investor makes a nice little profit on his investment. This system relies on the dollar remaining steady against the yen. So when the JPY/USD pair makes substantial moves in either direction, people will start to talk about yen carry traders.

The Swiss Franc

The Swiss franc, or Swissy and CHF, is the legal tender of Switzerland and Liechtenstein. The franc banknotes are issued by the Swiss National Bank, also known as the central bank of Switzerland; the coins are issued by the Swiss Federal Mint, Swissmint. The Swissy is the only version of the franc still issued in Europe. The most recent version of the Swiss franc was released in 1850.

The Swiss franc is hailed as a safe haven currency due to the history of political neutrality, the near zero inflation rate, and the historical legal requirement that at least 40% of the currency has been backed by gold reserves. The legal requirements regulating the currency to gold ratio were terminated in 2000 after an amendment to the Swiss Constitution.

The CHF has remained relatively stable against the euro since middle of 2003. It rises and falls against the U.S. dollar and is in line with the euro. Switzerland has remained a stable economy with a highly skilled labor force and a larger GDP per capita than other Western European economies. It also doesn't hurt that the unemployment has remained at less than half the EU average.

Chapter Four:
Fundamental Analysis
vs Technical Analysis

I am sure you have heard about both Fundamental and Technical Analysis, and now you are left pondering, "Which one works for me?" Everyone has their own opinion and will vehemently defend their view. My suggestion is to consider both in your daily trading. Technical analysts can point to example after example of why this type of analysis is the one you should use; but, if you have ever watched what happens to the markets on Non Farm Payroll Friday, then you cannot deny the power of Fundamental Analysis. See why I recommend that you consider both?

Let's take a closer look. You are trading on the first Friday of the month. Your chosen currency pair is in an uptrend, all your indicators say buy and the economic data comes in positive. You should feel confident about going long during the new announcement. You may even feel confident staying in your trade through the weekend and into the next week.

Now, if the trend is short, and the indicators are saying sell, but the economic data comes in positive, you may choose to go long during the news announcement, but will likely get out of this trade as soon as you make your desired profit. According to your technical analysis, the price is heading down, so you really shouldn't stay in over the weekend.

Limiting yourself to one style of analysis is a mistake. The more information you can gather regarding your currency pair, the better equipped you will be to trade in this highly volatile market.

Fundamental Analysis

Every time you hear someone talking about fundamental analysis in the Forex market you may notice that there is often very little information informing you how to perform your own fundamental analysis. Most traders (including myself) are left with questions like, "I don't get it, is there a PE ration of Japan?" Well, sort of. Fundamental analysis differs for the Forex market just a little bit, but some of the basic principles apply.

Fundamental analysis for the Forex market examines the macroeconomic indicators, asset markets, and political considerations of one nation's currency as opposed to another. Macroeconomic indicators include things such as: growth rates (Gross Domestic Product), interest rates, inflation, unemployment, money supply, foreign exchange reserves, and productivity. Other macroeconomic indicators include the CPI, a measurement of the cost of living, and the PPI, a measurement of the cost of producing goods. Asset markets are made up of stocks, bonds, and real estate. Political considerations influence the level of confidence in a nation's government, the climate of stability, and level of certainty.

There is a basic rule of thumb that says a currency can become more valuable in two main ways: when the amount of currency available in the world market place is reduced (for example, when the U.S. government raises the interest rates and causes a reduction in spending), or when there is an increase in the demand for that particular currency. But there are also many little things that can nudge the currency's value enough for the retail Forex trader to make (or lose) a substantial amount.

Let's take a moment to examine some of the fundamental information that has the potential to move the Forex market.

Getting a Bird's Eye View

If you want a solid view of the economy driving the currency pair you are trading, it is helpful to get a good overview of both currencies. One way to perform a more complete fundamental breakdown of a currency pair is to compile the following information:

Daily range (past x days):	Average:	Median:
Weekly range (past x weeks):	Average:	Median:

For each pair list:	Daily range	Weekly range
52 week high/low:		
Next Central Bank Meeting Date:		
GDP (annualized growth):		
Short term interest rate expectations:		
How are inflation rates?		
Unemployment rates:		

Filling out this form may help you examine the health of your chosen currency pair.

Checking Out the Macros

An interesting number to watch when you are checking out the macroeconomics of a country is the interest rate. Be careful not to jump to any premature decisions because, interest rates work like a split personality and can have both a strengthening and a weakening effect on your currency. On the negative side, investors will often sell off their holdings as interest rates increase because they believe that higher borrowing rates will adversely affect stock prices. This can cause a downturn in the stock market as well as in the national economy. High interest rates, however, tend to attract foreign investments, which strengthen the local currency.

Another thing to keep your eye on is the International Trade Balance. A trade balance that shows a deficit (more imports than exports) is usually a bad sign. Deficits mean that money is flowing out of the country to purchase foreign-made goods and this can have a devaluing effect on the currency. It is important to remember that the markets will generally dictate whether a trade deficit is bad news or not. If the country routinely operates with a deficit, it has probably already been factored into the currency price. Trade deficits will generally only affect a currency when they are reported higher than the market consensus.

The Asset Markets

The asset markets have an interesting tie to the value of a country's currency. For instance, in the past, the USD has moved in line with the stock markets. In fact, everywhere you look people are still touting that relationship. However, if you look at the charts, you will find that this doesn't really hold anymore. The trend lately has been if the stock markets are up, then the USD is usually down. This is possibly due to the fact that U.S. companies have increasingly derived their revenues from outside the U.S. You can also see the same sort of influences between the Japanese yen and the Nikkei.

Some currencies, however, are more closely aligned with the commodity prices. The four major currencies that are usually mentioned in conjunction with commodity prices are the Australian dollar, the Canadian dollar, the New Zealand dollar, and the Swiss franc. Gold and oil in particular, are the commodities that have the greatest influence on the Forex market and some tout them as leading indicators for Forex trading.

Watching the price of gold can be very beneficial for Forex traders, especially if you bear in mind that gold tends to move on inflationary scares. If you know how your chosen currency pair reacts to gold, you may have an interesting predictor of price movement.

For instance, the U.S. is the world's second largest producer of gold after South Africa. So, the price of gold can have a strong impact on the USD. It is important to remember, though, that gold doesn't normally move in line with the USD; they tend to have an inverse relationship to each other. The Australian dollar also has strong correlations with gold because Australia is the world's third largest exporter of gold. Bearing these facts in mind, it is easy to see why the AUD/USD pair tends to follow gold's price.

The other 800-pound commodity gorilla in the Forex market is oil. The Canadian dollar is the currency most influenced by rising or falling oil prices. If you have an eye for the USD/CAD, then it is interesting to watch oil-related news. For instance, several months ago, there was a spike in oil prices due to the death of a former Iraqi ruler. This spike translated into movements in the Forex markets. This was a classic example of using the price of oil as a leading indicator for Forex prices.

It's All About Politics

Politics can play a strong role in the value of a currency. Several misspoken words by a political leader can boost or drop that currency's value in a matter of seconds. A general rule of thumb is the more volatile the politics, the more volatile the currency. The political neutrality of the Swiss and the fact that a large amount of its currency reserves have traditionally been backed by gold is why the Swiss franc has been hailed as a safe haven during periods of uncertainty. This means that the CHF/USD ends up having a strong positive correlation with gold prices.

Technical Analysis: A Beginners Guide

Most people have heard of technical analysis. It has been around for well over 100 years and has been used heavily and touted by securities and commodity traders for decades. Many of us have been to a sales presentation advertising technical analysis. The charts flash up on the screen, the presenter points out perfect buy and sell signals, and at the end of the presentation, you are expected to shell out for a software program that will tell you exactly how to trade.

The fact is that you do not need to pay the big bucks to learn how to trade. Technical analysis is not hard or scary. Once you understand the basics, you will realize that there is a lot of information to be learned from your charts, and it is all free for the taking. Most of us have done a little technical analysis whether we know it or not. Just looking at a price chart is a rudimentary form of technical analysis.

Before we get started, however, I want to remind you that trading well is a skill that takes years of practice, a little training, and a lot of learning from past mistakes. I am not going to offer you a posy-lined path to market wisdom and success. To use a common analogy, there are many ways to build a house. You need to decide what kind of house suits you.

The Definition

The official definition of technical analysis is the analysis of past price data to determine future price movements. It is the study of prices in order to make better trades. The basis of modern-day technical analysis can be traced back to the Dow Theory, developed around 1900 by Charles Dow. It includes principles such as the trending nature of prices, confirmation and divergence, and support and resistance. Technical analysts, or chartists, use a number of tools to help them identify potential trades, some of which I will attempt to cover in this book.

Why Technical Analysis Works (Or Not)

Technical analysis uses past and current behavior to predict future behavior. Think of it like weather forecasting. The weatherman (or weatherperson, if you will) looks at the weather patterns that are currently emerging and compares them to similar weather patterns that have appeared in the past. If eight of the last ten instances of this weather pattern have produced rain, then the weatherperson can confidently predict rain.

Technical analysis works because humans are predictable. People often behave in predictable ways. They will consistently repeat their behavior under similar circumstances.

Technical analysis is the art and science of identifying crowd behavior in order to join the crowd and take advantage of its momentum. This is where the often-overused phrase "control your emotions" comes into play. You will want to be sensitive to what the market is doing without succumbing to crowd mentality. Technical traders work hard to avoid political and analyst chatter because they believe that all the information they need to know is already embedded in the price.

However, remember not to overanalyze; every action causes a reaction. There are millions of traders analyzing the same charts as you are and that leads to a cat-and-mouse sort of game playing that can be incredibly complex, riddled with bluffing, cheating feints, and double crosses. Traders can be a crafty bunch.

Components of Technical Analysis

Charts

Most technical analysts use charts as their primary tool. Charts are the heart and soul of the technical analysts tools, and they come in all shapes and sizes. The most commonly used types of charts are line, bar, candlestick, point and figure, and renko. Each price style has different interpretations and uses, and everyone has their favorites.

Trends

If I hear one more person say, "The trend is your friend," I will probably scream. Unfortunately, it is fairly apt, and you would be wise to remember that the trend does rule. There are countless books and articles out there that will tell you to trade with the trend. So we nod and smile and think, "Yes, I will always trade with the trend. That is completely logical." And they look so logical when you see someone else draw one on a chart. If you are like me, you think, "Of course! I would have to be a blithering idiot not to see the trend!" Then I go home and look at the chart and think, "Hmmm, is that an uptrend? Or perhaps it is a downtrend? Do I look at the one-hour chart or the 5-minute chart? What if they are different? Which low points do I use? And what about that weird spike?"

Identifying trends is a critical tool for the technical trader. The problem is figuring out how you will define a trend. I did a search on the Internet and found the following definitions for trend:

1. The general drift or tendency in a set of data;

2. The general direction, either upward or downward, in which prices have been moving;

3. The direction (either up, down or sideways) in which price and trading volume are moving over a short term or a long term basis;

4. The change in a series of data over a period of years that remains after the data has been adjusted to remove seasonal and cyclical fluctuations.

It seems to me that the definition of a trend is a little blurry. Even after you define trend, what type of trend are you talking about? Is it a major trend, a secular trend, a trend micro? For the sake of my sanity, let's define a trend as a series of higher highs or lower lows over a period of time, or the direction that the price is moving.

But charts don't always move in a nice smooth line in one direction or another. In fact, I have never seen a nice, smooth angled line. Price charts tend to zigzag back and forth along a general trend line. Trends have three basic directions: up, down, and sideways. Most of the tools on the market today have been designed for markets that are either moving up or down and tend to fail miserably when the market decides to move sideways; so, it is important to be able to monitor when the market has stagnated.

Trend Lines

Do you know how to draw your own trend lines? Do you know the definition? A trend line is defined as a straight line that starts at the beginning of the trend and stops at the end of the trend. Clear as mud, right? Pick the lowest lows in a move and draw a straight line connecting both the bottoms. Congratulations, there is your first trend line! The reason that you would want to draw a trend line is to help you identify places on your chart where the trend may change. That change isn't necessarily up to down. It can mean up to sideways, sideways to down, or any number of variations on the theme. So don't jump to conclusions if the price bars break the trend line. It could just mean a pause in the action before resuming the same trend path.

Drawing trend lines takes practice and confidence. First, look for the larger trend. If the chart is all over the place, then you will not be able to easily identify a solid trend, and while you are getting your feet wet, don't make yourself crazy. You will need two or three identifiable lows. Remember, it takes at least two points to draw a line. If you have only two points, don't count it as a firm trend line. Wait for the third bounce before you decide that it is truly a trend line. Once it has touched three times, you have a nice little trend line. This should hark back to your college physics classes and the old adage that a body in motion tends to stay in motion until acted upon by another force. The more times your price bounces off your trend line, the more significant you can consider your trend line to be.

Also, be realistic about whether a trend line is there or not. Often, you won't be able to draw trend lines on your chart. Remember, a valid trend line is a line that helps you identify the direction of a price move. Once you start drawing trend lines on your chart, you will be unable to stop. It is fascinating to watch a price move up and along the trend line, bouncing along like a rubber ball.

Once you get comfortable with your trend lines, start looking for breakouts. A breakout is any part of the price bar that penetrates a line that you drew on the chart. You will want to beware of false breakouts, though. False breakouts can be especially damaging because you may automatically want to assume that a breakout means a reversal. That is not necessarily true. But it is tempting to jump into a breakout because the first few periods after a breakout are often the best time to get in on the market move. In my experience, it seems to be that a breakout that occurs in the course of a low volatility trend is more likely to be meaningful than a breakout that occurs in a highly volatile trend.

You will need to experiment with your reactions to price penetrations of your trend lines. Some traders prefer to wait for the candle after the penetrating candle to make decisions regarding the validity of the penetration. You don't want to make a knee jerk decision and have the market return to its original path.

Check Appendix B for the Trend Line Workbook, complete with before and after charts. What I want you to do is break out your pencil and a straight edge and draw some trend lines.

Support and Resistance

Support and resistance lines are another valid concept that all technical traders respect. Think of prices as a head to head battle between the currencies in the pair you are trading. For instance, in the case of the EUR/USD, imagine the euro traders pulling one way and the USD trader pulling the other. The direction the price actually moves reveals who is winning the battle. Each time the price reaches a certain level, the euro traders will pull the euros' value back up and prevent it from falling further. This type of price action is called support because the euro traders are supporting the price. Similar to support, a resistance level is the point at which the sellers take control of the price and prevent them from rising higher. Support levels indicate the price where the majority of the investors believe prices will move higher, and resistance levels indicate the price at which the majority of investors feel prices will move lower.

You can identify support and resistance lines by drawing horizontal lines on your charts. It is always a good idea to know the support and resistance levels of the currency pair you are trading. The development of support and resistance levels is probably the most noticeable and recurring event on a price chart, and there may be places where you would want to put potential a stop-loss or take-profit. Penetration of these support and resistance levels leads to the formation of new support and resistance levels. The longer that the price remains at a support or resistance level, the more significant that level becomes.

Resistance Becomes Support and Vice Versa

When a resistance level is successfully penetrated, that level usually becomes a new support level. Similarly, when a support level fails, that level usually becomes a new resistance level.

Indicators

An indicator is a mathematical calculation that is applied to a security's price. The result is a value that is plotted on a chart and used to anticipate price changes. Or, in other words, lines and graphs that you can plot on your price charts to help you figure out what is happening.

There are literally thousands of indicators and many, many books that have been published about different indicators. I am not going to go into all the different indicators here, but I would advise you to keep it simple. There are four basic types of indicators: those that measure velocity, momentum, volatility, and volume. Volume doesn't hold in the Forex market because there isn't a central exchange that measures volume, but choosing one indicator from the remaining three categories should give you a balanced view of what is going on with your charts.

The heart of your chart watching and analysis should be your indicators. Everyone has their favorite indicators. I have seen many people sell their indicators for a pile of money. My opinion is that with a little perseverance, you can find pretty much any indicator you need on the Internet. So if you are willing to put in a little work, then you may find what you are looking for without shelling out hard earned cash. Remember that most "new and fabulous" indicators are really just regular indicators with a few tweaked settings that someone has changed the name on in order to solicit a bunch of sales. You are better off doing a little homework and understanding what your charts are trying to tell you.

For a quick review of common indicators see Appendix A.

Convergence and Divergence

You will hear these two terms often when you listen to the market analysts. Convergence refers to two indicator lines coming closer to one another and divergence refers to two indicator lines moving farther apart. Convergence is most often seen in indicators on the price chart, and generally means that the price action is starting to go sideways or has a narrower high-low range.

Benchmark Levels

Benchmark levels refer to the historic highs and lows on a price chart. These aren't indicators that can be applied to a chart but may serve to indicate future price action. When a price makes a new historic high or low and then retraces, it can be quite some time before the benchmark is surpassed. Historic levels can cause some strange indicator behavior. If an uptrending indicator flattens out mysteriously, widen the timeframe on your chart to see whether the price is near a historical level. The market will test these historical levels. If the test fails, then you might expect a retracement and perhaps a reversal.

Retracements

Admitting that no one can forecast a retracement hasn't stopped many people from trying. The following guidelines are helpful but don't statistically sound, so proceed with caution.

- A retracement won't usually exceed a significant prior high or low.

- Watch for round numbers. Traders are human and as people we tend to like nice round numbers. Think about it, would you set a stop at 1.2527 or 1.2530?

- The 30 percent rule: you can assume that a majority of traders will place stops to avoid losing more than a certain percentage, like 30%. The only issue with this is that you don't know where the majority of traders got into the market.

Noted technician, W.D. Gann used to say that the best retracement was a 50 percent retracement. It is the best place to re-enter an existing trend. If the trend resumes, it will then exceed the previous high, which identifies an immediate minimum profit target.

Fibonacci

Fibonacci numbers were named after Leonardo of Pisa, also known as Fibonacci, even though they had already been described earlier in India. The best-known Fibonacci numbers are a simple series of numbers that form a sequence. After two starting values, zero and one, each number is the sum of the two preceding numbers. The Fibonacci numbers are studied as part of number theory and have applications in the counting of mathematical objects such as sets, permutations, and sequences. Fibonacci levels are commonly placed on charts to predict potential retracement levels.

Market scholar, Ralph Nelson Elliot, believed that those Fibonacci numbers could also be found in man's behavior and could therefore be charted to predict future behavior. Elliott observed that securities prices appear in a wave like form on charts, hence the name Elliott Waves. Elliott wave adherents often use Fibonacci levels, with special attention to the 38 percent and 62 percent levels, to predict the extension of the retracements.

Chapter Five:
Making or Breaking News

If you haven't seen the movie *Fight Club* you may miss this reference, but that's all right. Just remember, there are two roles in Trade Club:

1. The market doesn't make any sense,

2. Even when it seems like it is making sense, the market doesn't make any sense.

As we already know, there are two camps in the analysis world: the technical people and the fundamental people. I come from a primarily technical background; but, since my induction into the Forex market, I have been dabbling more and more in the fundamental side as well. You really can't be a Forex trader for more than five minutes (especially on the first Friday of every month) without being impacted by news and economic data in one way or another.

Recently, I noticed the EUR/USD heading down to that lovely support level of 1.270 and decided to go long (in a big way). I had been pretty successful trading that pair in the 1.270–1.290 range and figured it would be heading back towards the top and I could cash in big. One day later, the euro was looking even better at 1.2675 and, being overconfident like I am, I went long again.

Then along comes Non Farm Payroll Friday. Let me digress here and talk about fundamental news announcements. There are tons of you crazy news traders out there. You sit there with your finger on the mouse, hyped up on adrenaline like news junkies. The market during news times is wildly unpredictable. Let's face it; you thrive on the thrill of the hunt. Personally, I am a chicken. I don't like watching the news; it makes me tense. Plus, I think that the market is insane.

Getting back to Non Farm Friday, the consensus of that particular Friday was for between 120k – 125k. I had been to all the news websites and had read all the analysts predictions, then I wake up Friday morning and see that the actual number is 51k. 51k! This has to mean doom for the USD right? Unemployment is a mere 0.1% lower than expected and hourly earnings are 0.1% lower than expected. This is BAD data for the USD. So, extremely pleased, I opened my charts. Within an hour's time, the EUR/USD had dropped below 1.26 into the 1.25 range. Every analyst on the web had a different opinion on why this was the case (most of which I thought were crazy).

Let's take a look at the cold hard facts:

Oct 3 – Buy the EUR/USD 1.2734

Oct 5 – Buy the EUR/USD 1.2711

Oct 6 – Non Farm Consensus 120k, Actual 51k.

Shortly after Non Farm, the EUR/USD is at 1.2598.

Buy the EURUSD at 1.2671. I know, I know… don't keep buying on the way down. Here I go again, trading like a girl. My thought process goes like this: "Oh! The euro is on sale! I will buy some." and "Oh, the euro has been discounted further! I will buy some more!" and so on.

Oct 11 – FOMC (Federal Open Market Committee) Minutes. Boy I was hoping Bernake would say something and send the market into a tailspin. No such luck. EUR/USD at 1.2497. Now I am starting to sweat.

Oct 12 – Trade Balance Consensus -$66.5B. Actual -$69.9B. "Beautiful", I think. "This HAS to be bad." EUR/USD at 1.2519. Not bad enough, I guess.

Oct 13 – Friday the 13th has always been a lucky day for me so I had high hopes.

Retail sales consensus 0.1%, actual -0.4%

Ex-auto consensus 0.0%, actual -0.5%

Mich Seniment – Prel. Consensus 86.5, actual 92.3

Business Inventories – consensus 0.5%, actual 0.6%

EUR/USD now at 1.2482

At this stage I admit I am stumped. I have been given a dozen different explanations and personally, I think they are all rubbish.

Oct 17 – PPI consensus -0.7%, actual -1.3%

Net Foreign Purchases consensus $53.0B, actual $116.8B

Industrial Production consensus -0.1%, actual -0.6%

Capacity Utilization consensus 82.2%, actual 81.9%

EUR/USD at 1.2552

Oct 18 & 19 – pretty good data for the U.S.

Housing Starts consensus 1650k, actual 1772k

Initial Claims consensus 310k actual 299k

EUR/USD at 1.2603

We are now sitting on a resistance level that used to be support. Personally, I am hoping for a good push through so I can regain some dignity and equity. I believe fundamental announcements can and do move the markets in dramatic ways. I also believe that technicals play a large part in this game because let's face it, when you sit down and look at it, sometimes the market just doesn't make any sense.

I did eventually recover from this shopping spree and while I don't recommend trading like a girl and try to refrain from trading like a girl myself, sometimes a good sale is just too interesting to pass up.

So, You Want to Trade the News

There seems to be a lot of hype around trading fundamental news announcements in the Forex market lately. In my opinion, that is due to two reasons: 1) a number of brokers have recently decided to stop allowing trading during news; and 2) the number of people touting trading the news as the best way of making money in Forex seems to be growing.

Let me expound just a little as I roll my eyes. I have now read the 1,000th article by some so-called guru selling something that essentially states, "Timing your trades in the Forex market can be difficult. But if you look at the fundamental news announcements you will see large potentials for gain." There is usually an accompanying chart complete with a lovely arrow at the time of the news announcement, a couple of huge candles immediately after the lovely green arrow, and quite often in big letters something inflammatory like, "Over 100 Pips!"

It is so easy to look at a historical chart and point out buy and sell points. It looks impressive. And to those who don't understand the dangers and pitfalls laying ahead, it looks like a no brainer. Why would you trade at any other time when there is all this fabulous money to be made during news announcements?

If nothing else sinks in, I would like to advise you to please, please not trade the news. It takes a lot of experience, nerves of steel, and quite a lot of discipline. It is not for everyone and certainly not for those who don't fully understand all the ramifications of news trading. Rather, you should be aware of the news, put your time into knowing how the market affects your chosen currency pair(s), and understand how the numbers in each news report relate to its market price and movements.

What Exactly Happens To The Market?

The currency market is faster and more volatile than any other market out there. However, during high volatility times, like news announcements, it can perform unbelievable feats. Generally called "fast market" by most brokers, these high volatility times can bring wild swings in the currency prices, enormous price gaps, widening spreads, and millions of transactions happening all at the same time.

My definition of a price gap is when the price of a currency pair either jumps or falls from its last bid, or ask quote, to a new quote, never trading at the prices in between these two prices. When this happens, both stop-loss and entry-stop orders will either be executed at their requested rate (if the market happened to trade there) or at the next recorded price in the market. This is an important point, which we will come back to shortly.

In fast market instances, both stop-loss and entry-stop orders will either be executed at their requested rate (if the market happens to trade there), or at the next recorded price in the market, regardless of order size. These prices may be substantially different from your requested rate.

The standard industry practice for most currency dealers (including dealers in the Interbank market) during fast market conditions is to set market levels and execute orders manually without the use of automated systems or services. During fast markets, the process is generally as follows:

- Initially, major money center banks and other online price providers halt all direct dealing and their pricing engines are suspended.

- Currency dealers analyze the event and determine the correct price.

- Prices enter the markets 20 -30 Pips wide or more.

- Spreads in the market narrow as more currency dealers enter the market.

During a fast market event, there are typically delays in trade execution, which may be significant, while rates are cross-referenced to ensure valid execution. Stops placed close to a market that has traded through the stop price can be repriced on the next best tradable price. Thereby, a specified rate order does not provide a fixed-price guarantee to the news trader or broker.

What does all that mean? Basically it means that just before a news event, you will notice spreads widen. Immediately after the event, prices vary widely and all pending orders and stop-losses become market orders and get filled at the next available price. Spreads remain wide as long as it takes for the news event to settle and trading returns to normal.

The Players

Now that we have identified how the market works in fast market conditions, let's look at the traders who typically trade in this game. Note that each of these traders face different, and no less dangerous, pitfalls. The bulk of the people that I see trading the news fall into one of three categories:

The Quick Clicker

This trader subscribes to a good, fast news service and trades just after the news announcement has been released and (hopefully) before the market has had time to react. The quick clickers of the world usually spend the big bucks for a fast, reliable data feed. They wait for the actual announcement with their mouse between the buy and the sell buttons. They generally have already decided which way they will trade depending on the actual release numbers.

This trader faces a number of dangers, lagging execution being one of the most talked about. If you follow this method and your broker allows market orders, you will be filled at the next available price. This means you may be filled at a substantially different price than the one on the screen when you clicked the button. In one case, about three years ago, there was a 50 Pip gap during a Non Farm Payroll announcement. If your broker is not a market maker, you may also see a widening of the spreads right at the announcement time. While your pair may only have a 2 Pip spread in normal market conditions, you may have to cover eight, ten or more Pips before your trade is profitable. Fortunately (or not), the markets tend to move extremely quickly during these times, so you may quickly cover the difference or alternately show a resounding loss that much quicker.

The Quick Clicker and the Strategist also face ramifications from banks and brokers alike. This is commonly referred to as flagging. If the trader consistently trades large lots for short time periods during news times, he runs the risk of additional interference from the banks. Known as scalping, trading this way on a consistent basis is frowned upon. Traders should trade during non-news times as well as news times and try to hold their trades for longer periods. Gaining redemption after being flagged is not always an easy thing to do and can cause you problems down the road.

The Strategist

This trader straddles the market hoping to catch the move no matter which direction it moves. The Strategists' concepts seem logical. Place a buy-limit (complete with stop-losses) and a sell-limit (also complete with stop-losses). The issue here has to do with market volatility and the widening on the spread. For example, let's say the bid of the EUR/USD is at 1.2867 with a spread of 2. You place a buy limit at 1.2880 with a stop-loss at 1.2865, and a sell limit at 1.2857 with a stop-loss of 15. A currency pair can whipsaw wildly when an announcement happens. In a matter of a few minutes, the pair can bounce around like a water droplet on a hot pan. So, the market jumps up to 1.2889, where you get filled; remember, buy-limits may not hold and you might get filled at the next available price. It then bounces straight back down. To be fair, let's say it trades at your stop-loss price and you only lose 24 Pips. It can continue straight down and trigger your sell at 1.2857. We will be nice and fill at that price even though that may or may not happen in real life. We will also assume that you get out where you want, only losing an additional 15 Pips. So, in the space of seconds you have lost 39 Pips. Suddenly your grand idea looks more like a guaranteed way to get completely whipsawed and drop your account balances. We didn't even factor in the widening of the spreads. If the spreads move from 2 to 10 Pips, your pending orders and stop-loses will be executed that much quicker.

The Wait and See

This trader waits for the dust to settle and tries to catch the retracements. They tend to avoid the bulk of the stress and hassle tied to fast market conditions. They wait for the dust to settle a bit and then try to catch a little profit when the pair is on it's way back from where it came, whether it is over the course of minutes or days. Because they get in after the market has progressed through the bulk of the fast market behavior, their trades are generally executed fairly quickly, though they may experience some slippage and slower execution speeds than normal market conditions. The Wait and See trader also runs the risk that the currency pair will not retrace at all but find a new support or resistance level where it ended up.

So, You Still Want To Trade The News?

So now you know the dangers of trading the news. If you are determined to trade the news, I would suggest that you have sufficient funds in your account before you place any trade; getting caught in a margin call during news announcements just adds insult to injury. Also, be aware that your market order executions may be significantly different from the price you were quoted during market fluctuations. Here is where I would like to interject Marilyn's Little News Trading Rules. They may help to keep your account from a margin call if you decide to get involved with news trading.

Rule #1—*Know Your News.* Find out which news events are going to impact your relationship with your trade. Some news releases will be a small blip on your radar screen, while others will equal a tsunami! Mark the tsunami dates on your calendar. Some of the coolest economic calendars I have seen will allow you to download your important events directly into your Outlook or handheld. Information is power; and, if you know something whacky is coming around the bend, the better chance you have of getting out with your account intact.

Rule #2—*Get In Or Get Out.* So you know a news event is coming and you are already in a position. Is this a long-term position? Do you truly believe that your chosen currency will continue on in a manner you have predicted after the news? Now is the point that you have to ask yourself some hard questions. If you decide that you are in for the long haul, then you need to maintain your course. If you are simply playing in the short term, then you need to either stay in or get out. Make a hard choice and live with it. I know you would like someone to tell you what to do but let's face it, how can anyone tell you what you should do? So, are you up 20 Pips on 1 lot? Have you bet the kid's college fund? By the way, I do NOT recommend this. Only trade with money that you would be fine with losing. Pick and don't look back.

Rule #2—*Cover Your Assets.* Make sure you have enough margin in your account so that if the trade goes against you, your broker isn't going to start knocking you out of your trades. The last thing you want is a really bad trade draining your account, causing a margin call, and then having the price retrace exactly back to where you thought it would go. So, have a close look at your charts and make some predictions of where you think the price will go. You can set up hedges, trailing stops, or stop-losses, but make sure you carefully examine your charts and your ability to either ride out a bad loss, or at what stage you will be satisfied and take the profit.

Rule #4—*Calculate the Drama.* Here is a tough one. It is extremely hard to predict what the market is going to do during a news event. I know mathematicians that spend hours and hours trying to calculate the impact of a "Standardized Unexpected Event." I found all the calculations incredibly hard to process, and in the end I didn't see the point of some of it. (I know I will take some heat for this. Just you watch, those mathematicians that I know are going to rail on for hours about being on the right side of the trade. It all looks like an extremely complex set of moving averages to me, and half of the time, the predictions are just as random as everything else I have seen about predicting news announcements.) Some economic calculators will have a rating system that will give you an idea of what kind of impact the news announcement could possibly have on your chosen currency pair.

Now, More News!

As you have probably now realized, Non Farm Payroll is the granddaddy of all news announcements. Fortunes can be won and lost in a matter of a minutes on that first Friday of each month. However, there are other news announcements that can move the market in less dramatic but in no less profitable ways.

Let's have a quick look at the numbers behind the USD and see if we can't find some other news announcements to follow and perhaps trade.

The first thing to realize is that no single economic indicator will tell you all you need to know; however, knowledge is power, so it is wise to arm yourself with as many weapons as possible. Since most of the currency pairs I trade include the USD, I keep my eye on the 12 indicators that underscore the health of the U.S. economy. I call these my secondary news announcements, and they can and do influence my trading. They are worth keeping your eyes on if you are trading a USD pair.

1. GDP
2. Indices of Leading, Lagging, and Coincident Indicators
3. The Employment Situation
4. Industrial Production and Capacity Utilization
5. Institute for Supply Management Indices
6. Manufacturer's Shipments, Inventories, and Sales
7. Manufacturing and Trade Inventories and Sales
8. New Residential Construction
9. Conference Board Consumer Confidence and University of Michigan Consumer Sentiment Indices
10. Advance Monthly Sales for Retail Trade and Food Services
11. Personal Income and Outlays
12. Consumer and Producer Price Indices

You can learn more about all of these news announcements in *More News to Trade* found in Appendix D.

The Final Headline

As you will find out, watching the news quickly becomes an all consuming hobby for the fundamental news trader. Headlines like "Fed Futures

Start to Price in Rate Cuts," "4% Chance of Oct. Easing," and "Odds of 41% by Jan 31 as Weak Philly Fed Index Spurs Fear of Big Slowing" should make you sit up and take a look if you are trading a pair that is influenced by the USD. This sort of news will typically impact the U.S. stock markets, which will influence the Forex market.

In contrast, headlines like "Energy Prices Keeping Cooling Off" should make you take a look at the Canadian dollar, as its value fluctuates in correlation to oil. In fact, let's take it a step further. Let's say there is some political event that spikes (up or down) the price of oil. This will have an impact on the Canadian dollar, and most of the time there is a bit of a lag. This means there is time to take advantage of the movement.

Fundamental information can be just as influential on your trading as technical analysis. When you understand the information behind the news regarding your chosen currencies, you will be able to trade more confidently when news and politics move the market. Watch all signs with an open mind. When you have a currency pair and commodity that moves closely in line with each other, either one can lead; you should be watching for moves in both.

Another interesting phenomenon to watch is the market's reaction to fundamental news. If the news is bullish and the market fails to react in an overbought area, then you should be watching for a turn in the trend. The next advent of adverse news should be enough to turn the tide.

Take a look at the types of news announcements that can affect the markets in Appendix D.

Chapter Six:
Automated Trading

As we all now know, the Forex markets can jump around like a squirrel on speed, and it's open for trading 24 hours a day.   So, it's pretty much impossible for any one trader to take advantage of every trading opportunity that happens during market hours, unless of course you are (or employ) a machine. This desire to trade around the clock is spawning a market-wide interest in automated trading, or as I like to call it "The Rise of The Machine."

The trading industry has long focused on providing their customers with strategies. Take any major trading software and you will find a slew of "plug-ins" and "add-ons," with the names of Elliot Waves, Bollinger Bands, Candlestick Patterns, and many others. These add-ons will display signals and sometimes recommendations on the end user's charts. An investor still has to pull the trigger, though. The program only goes as far as telling you what to trade and what stop-loss and profit target to use, but never actually executes the trade. In the last few months, far more attention has been given to automated trading. Only a handful of trading platforms currently offer this technology. I personally use Interbank FX Trader 4.

What is Automated Trading?

Automated Trading is the ability to let your computer place trades based on your trading strategy. In Interbank FX Trader 4, automated trading is done through what we call an "Expert Advisor," which is the program you attach to a chart that executes trades for you. The machine isn't infallible; there are a few limitations.

The Expert Advisor relies on your computer to be running and connected to the Internet.

You should also take measures to prevent power failures, disconnects, and other computer-related problems. Don't worry too much; just take some basic precautions with a few simple fail-safes.

First and foremost, your Expert Advisor has to be programmed. If you are not a programmer, do not despair. Many are available for hire. Whether you have some basic programming knowledge or not, I highly recommend that you do take some time and try to learn the language. Many tutorials and sample codes are available all over the Internet.

Why Use Automated Trading?

No matter how you first learned about trading, you will come across the same, overworked idioms:

- Do not use emotions in your trading, namely greed and fear.
- Always set a stop loss and a profit target.
- Execute trades quickly.

Bear all these in mind, take some time, and think through your trading system carefully. Then, think through the system again. Carefully considering all the possible outcomes is key to the best possible system. Your Expert won't make adjustments for market volatility, nor will it take every eventuality into consideration unless you have already thought every scenario through and made decisions about what you would like your

Expert to do. On the other hand, an Expert Advisor will not modify a stop-loss because it believes the market will turn around and try to give its trade one last chance (subsequently breaking the bank). Nor will it modify the profit target of a trade because suddenly it thinks it can make more money. The execution is done within seconds; the program won't second-guess itself. It sees a signal and it places the trade.

There are other interesting facets to automated trading. It is not just about eliminating counter-productive emotions. If you have been in the Forex game for any length of time, you know as well as I do that some nights you have a hard time sleeping. You have placed that one trade that can bring you riches or kill your account and are up fretting and watching charts in a cold house with scratchy eyes. With an Expert Advisor attached to your chart, you sleep without a care knowing that your program can identify trading opportunities and set trailing stops and profit targets. No more late nights spent worrying about your trades.

This brings up yet another advantage. You are trading while sleeping, yet your strategy could trigger many signals and make a profit during times you could not trade before. You are no longer limited by that pesky need to eat, sleep, and socialize with the family.

Another interesting benefit of employing a computer in your trading is that you can program your Expert to scan for opportunities on any and all available currency pairs and periodicities. You will no longer need to open 15 charts to make sure you don't miss out on a good trade; an Expert Advisor can make sure you see any available opportunity and trade them for you.

Automated Trading has brought to light new strategies that would never have worked in the past, due to human limitations. Trading is often compared to gambling at a casino, except in trading you can improve your odds by using technical analysis. Well, in the same vein, let's use the saying "the house always wins." It always wins because it is always playing; all the losses are outdone by the wins. In theory, if you had a strategy with 51% accuracy, you traded for small profits/losses (a few Pips, and I'm not referring to scalping here), and traded very often (hundreds of trades a day), then you would (in theory) make money every day. Only a computer program could execute and manage these hundreds of trades for you every day.

How To Write an Expert Advisor

How does one write an automated strategy? A big mistake made by new-bies and seasoned traders alike is to look for an expert that was created by some other party and try to see if it makes money or matches their own strategy. I personally think of an automated expert not as my replace-ment or a money making machine, but more as my backup or substitute. If I can't trade for any reason (sleeping, working, shopping, etc.), then I will let my trusty substitute go in for me.

I say it is a mistake for newbies because they do not try to learn how to trade on their own, therefore, do not understand the signals they get on their screen. It must feel to them like some stranger is interfering with their trading account. "Hey who is trading my account? What kind of trade is that? I don't get it." If you don't want to take the time to under-stand why you should be placing a given trade, I would think you would be better off using a money manager for your account rather than try to use some "highly acclaimed" expert found on some forum.

This is a mistake for a seasoned trader because by now, he or she should know better. A seasoned trader should already have a few indicators and a few techniques he or she is familiar and comfortable with. They may not realize it but they already are using a system; they just need to logi-cally think through all the eventualities and then program it.

What most programmers would tell anyone interested in automating their strategy is to write down why they placed a trade on paper. Keep a journal of your trades for maybe a month. See what trades were good and which were not, but most importantly, record why a trade was entered. What did you see on the chart that made you say, "I'm buying this many lots of this currency pair and will set the following stop-loss and profit-target." Every detail counts.

The programming languages are powerful and very flexible. You can decide to only trade during specific hours and days. I even know of people who have created experts based of moon cycles. Nothing is impossible as long as you can specifically define it. Recently, news trading has become very popular. Some programmers have created experts to read a text file containing the dates and time of news announcements and have used that to trigger trades. Although it can be very complex, quite frankly, more complex than I think is necessary, I truly believe that most strategies can be programmed.

How To Test the Expert Advisor

So now that you have your expert and have programmed it (or someone did it for you), it is time to put it to the test. Many platforms will provide you with a "back tester" or a "simulator" of some sort. In my opinion, these should be called "debuggers" but we will come back to this later. So you run your simulation and get a fabulous little report. Regardless of what the final numbers say (whether or not you have made an imaginary profit), I recommend you only look at the trades. Did it place the entry and exit points according to your strategy? If not, spend some time adjusting the code to fix the errors and stop looking at the profit. That brings up a common pitfall for programmers: curve fitting. Do not get lured by some extraordinary results; stay the course and stick to your original design. The same goes with bad results: do not just give up on your Expert Advisor because the back tester's results look really bad. At this point in the design process, you should only focus on getting entry and exit signals to match your original strategy, nothing else. Do not waste your time optimizing and curve fitting. It'll only end in tears.

Once you have checked the signals and they are accurate, your expert is ready. Now it is time to do a real test. Most Forex brokers will let you download a demo account. My recommendation is to open such a demo account and let your expert trade live for a month or so. No matter how great a platform claims their back testing or simulations to be, nothing will be as good as the real thing. Run the strategy live on a dummy account. That is why I ask people not to waste time curve fitting their systems, and why I call the "back tester" the debugger. Its only use should be to check that the signals are accurate. The only people who care about simulation results are businesses who are trying to sell you an add-on and are trying to prove it works.

You will continue to hear more and more about automated trading. It can be a tremendous tool to help you in your trading, but as with everything, you will need to do your homework. Never forget, though, that a tool cannot replace you nor should you expect it to. You need to remain in charge of your trading.

Chapter Seven:
Mentally Preparing To Trade

One of the first things you need to do before you place your trades is to determine exactly what you want to achieve. Get out a piece of paper and write it down. Do you want to eventually live off your trading? Or are you just trying to outperform your 401k or Money Market account? Be as specific as you can and then pin this up by your computer.

When you sit down to trade each day take four or five minutes and review your goals before you start clicking that mouse. This will help you keep your goals in mind as you trade. If your goal is to make 20 pips per day then you will start each trading day with that particular goal in mind. It is easy to get wrapped up in the emotion of the moment and forget your larger picture. Taking a few minutes before the day starts will help you focus on your goals.

Be aware that when you start trading you may be confronted by negativity from your friends or relatives. They simply don't understand what you are doing or the language you are now learning. Some people react to new situations with fear and frustration. You may need to join a traders group, whether it be online or in person. Make sure you have friends and associates that understand the new language you speak and can possibly help you learn from your mistakes.

Remain focused. Every new trader will hit a wall. They will become overconfident and lose a lot of money, potentially even their entire account. This usually comes after a series of wins. The true test of your character as a trader is going to be what you do with yourself after this happens. Do you quit? Or do you dust yourself off and build on the hard lessons that you have learned? Your actions at this stage of the game are going to help form what kind of trader you will grow to be. My advice for this situation is to lean on your fellow traders. Anyone who has been in the market for any length of time has been through this. This is what separates the men from the boys (so to speak).

If you are having emotional responses to your trades, it is time to pay attention. During these times, walk away from your computer if you can. When you lose your emotional detachment, you have lost your perspective. You are now far more likely to place bad trades, second guess yourself, and close out everything at a loss. Take a break, get out of the house, and come back when you can look at the charts and your account impassively.

Beware of greed. This is one of the seven deadly sins for a reason. Greed can cause you to act impulsively and irrationally. Set your goals for the trading session, achieve your goals, and be grateful for another day of trading successfully.

Track your progress. As long as you can see that you are progressing down your projected path then you will continue to stick to your trading plan. This also gives you the confidence you need to see that your plan is working. Don't deviate from your plan, remain steadfast and you can achieve your goals. Think slow and steady and you will maintain your trading edge.

The bottom line here is to enjoy trading for what it is, trading. It is taking a risk, placing a trade, and watching to see if your analysis was correct. The fact is, trading is interesting and while you might not get into the market to learn about economics and world events, you may just walk away with a world-class education.

Be Sure to Check Your Emotions at the Door

So, on Wednesday night you are trading and you can do no wrong. By Friday you are sobbing in your coffee and lamenting your idiocy. What are you doing to yourself? You started off not taking life too seriously and trading your mini account (or perhaps that standard account). If you gain $100 or lose $100, it wasn't really all that big of a deal. Then, somewhere along the line, your account built up to the point (or was reduced to the point) that it started to really matter to you. Making money on that one trade was suddenly very important. From that point on, you are blowing trades left, right, and center. Have you lost your charm, the thing that made you golden?

Not true. What you have lost is not your charm, it is your common sense, your sense of detachment. Now, it's personal. Those crazy emotions start kicking in (remember those) and you are making decisions that you would not have made before.

Emotions are Big Business

Everywhere I look, people are talking about the emotions in trading. There are seminars about how to eliminate your emotions and coaches to teach you how to deal with you emotions. Go to any trader's expo and that is one of the points that people talk about endlessly. Do a Google search on trading psychology. You are going to find books, systems, training, and all sorts of stuff. When I did this search, most of the first page listings were people selling systems based on trading psychology. There aren't too many people out there who actually want to help you deal with your emotions.

The reality is you can't help but get emotional. I promise this will happen to you—you will make a couple of bad trades and will fret over it ceaselessly. Or, you will make a couple of good trades and strut around like a god among mortals. Read what you like, attend those hideously expensive seminars, but at some stage in your first couple of days, weeks and months of trading, you are going to feel invincible. My husband, Patrick, is one of the most levelheaded people I know. He has written trading systems, trading strategies, and endless indicators for companies and individual traders over the years. He has read most of the books by the experts and has publicly stated that most of them say the same things (create your own plan, devise your own strategy) and then at the end of the book they contradict themselves and ask you to buy their system.

Yet, he is as human as the rest of us and thought he was invincible after his first few weeks in the Forex market. He was particularly crazed after his first Non-Farm Payroll Friday. As of this writing I am still waiting for the bubble to burst, not that I want to see him suffer or lose money. It's just that he has become a little insufferable.

So, what can you do? Well, acknowledging that this is going to happen to you will help. Try to identify an emotional high or low while it is happening. I have a little rule that I like to enforce. I only allow myself three open trades. I might see a fourth setting up but I don't let myself take another trade without closing out one of my other open trades. Have I missed out? Probably, however, this has also saved my backside when I have gone into a shopping frenzy. See, sometimes I too think I am invincible.

Also, don't kick yourself when you are down. Remember, it is expected that less than 15% of all Forex traders are successful. So if you win eight out of every ten trades, you are beating the odds, right? I can win three out of four trades. That one that I lose makes me pout insufferably. What I have learned to do is just deal with it, sort my head out, and get back into the game.

What About Using a Managed Account?

Maybe you've gotten this far and have decided that perhaps you would be better off putting some funds into a managed account rather than trading actively yourself. This is a hard decision, and if you have self- examined and reached this point, then I applaud your honesty. The following are some nuggets of advice that may help you choose a money manager.

Rule #1: Don't Let Your Friend Trade Your Account

Seriously, this one should be as sacred as don't lend money to your friends. If the funds exchange hands, you would have to consider it a gift. If you get it back, then be grateful. If not, well you never really expected it back anyway, so no need to fret.

Some of the most confused and upset people I have come across are ones who have had friends trade their accounts. It doesn't quite compute that this person, whom they probably have dinner with, invite to social occasions, and let their kids play with, has lost their money or at least a fair chunk of it. And you know it is hard for the friend to tell everyone, "Hey, I made some spectacularly bad trades for you. I have lost my behind and so did you. If you hang in there with me, I will try to get it back for you."

Rule #2: Ask for More Information

As I mentioned earlier, why does someone who does stringent due diligence when it comes to financing their car, opening a bank account, or getting a credit card suddenly lose their mind when it comes to choosing someone to trade their Forex account? Rather than logically evaluating money managers, asking for substantiation on earnings claims, and just generally checking these people out, they randomly toss money to the biggest hucksters and then complain loudly when these accounts go into a free fall. "It must be an accounting problem!" "The broker has a problem with their software." Wake up and smell the declining equity line. The problem is that your choice of money managers was not well thought out and you took claims on face value.

If you choose wisely, by following these two simple rules, a managed account might be the right choice for you.

Final Warning, Forex is Not for Everyone

If you want to see people squirm uncomfortably, then talk to them about the risks associated with Forex trading. This is one of those "elephant in the middle of the room" moments. No one really wants to point it out but everyone is alluding to its presence. I have seen the pitches:

We offer 400:1 leverage!

Forex is more lucrative because you are trading on margin!

The truth is that Forex trading is risky, very risky. You can make money very quickly. However, you can also blow up your entire account (and sometimes more) just as easily. And it's not just you that can lose your shirt. If you have been interested in Forex for more than a few weeks, you will recall the headlines:

21st Century Bank Run

Watching a $4 Billion Company Fall Apart in a Week

When you open your demo account (which you should definitely do), you will notice that the Forex market can jump around like a squirrel on speed. The speed and volatility of this market can and will kick you in the pants if you are not careful. This unpredictable nature is what attracts investors to trade in the currency market.

So, what are the risks you will be facing? Well, you may see things like:

- unexpected fluctuations in exchange rates,
- volatile market swings due to news or nothing perceivable at all.

This may seem daunting but there are things that you can do to limit your risk.

Watch Your Leverage

I actually had someone tell me, "I will not trade with your brokerage because I need the 400:1 leverage." I was shocked. Why would someone need 400:1 leverage? The higher the leverage, the higher the risks. With most brokers out there you can choose your leverage amount. Typically you will see 100:1 or 200:1; however, I know traders that use 20:1 or even no leverage at all. To drop to that level you will need to have a fairly large amount of risk capital.

Let's take a closer look at leverage. In order to trade $100,000 with no leverage, you would need $100,000; with 100:1 leverage, you would only need $1,000 in your margin account to trade this amount. With 200:1 leverage you would only need $500. The potential for making money is much higher, however, so is the potential for loss. My advice to you is not to go stupid with leverage. It really isn't worth it in the long run.

Set Profit Targets and Limit Your Losses

I like to make 10 or 15 or even 20 pips and get out. Do I miss out on some terrific moves? You bet! Do I make a profit while some people lose everything they have gained due to retracements? You bet! I am happy making a bit of money and getting out. I don't get too greedy because it makes me nervous. Decide how much you think it will go up or how much will make you happy and set that take-profit level.

Setting a stop-loss will allow you to decide how much you want to lose. This is a tough decision because if you set it too close in volatile conditions, the market is likely to dip down, bump you out of your trade, and reverse back up to make a profit. However, a stop loss will save your behind if you simply read the market wrong and make a bad decision.

There are plenty of websites out there willing to tell you where to place your take- profit and stop- loss orders. I am not going to go there. I will simply default to my mantra: read everything you can get a hold of, try it out on a demo account, and then make your own decisions.

Chapter Eight:
Make Your Plan

Now it is time for you to decide what and when you will trade. It is time for you to develop your trading plan. Please don't put your faith and hard earned dollars into some black box system that is more likely than not just a moving average cross system. It is important for you to know why you are placing the trades you are. If you are not willing to put some work into creating your own trading plan, I think it would be more beneficial for you to place your money into a managed account, simply to give it a fighting chance in this challenging arena.

The first step in making your own trading plan is to put in the hard work and develop your own trading style—not mine, or some suit's from a presentation, or even a slick website salesman. When you set out to define your trading style, it needs to be yours and yours alone.

Developing a trading plan is very similar to a company business plan. It is a device for you to define how you intend to operate your business. A trading plan lays out how you will make trades; the time, price, volume, and news are all essential components of the trade. While your trading plan may not necessarily be for others, it is still your own road map to tell yourself, and reaffirm to yourself, how you expect to get there. Include goals in your plan: three-month, six-month, one-year, two-years, five-years, ten-years, and beyond.

Elements to Consider

- What times during the day will you be trading (which sessions)?

- What currency pairs are you interested in following?

- Will you be trading during volatile market moves (fundamental news announcements)?

- How long will you hold your trades?

- How much are you willing to risk in the markets?

Essentials of a Trading Plan

There are many essentials you may want to consider in your trading plan. These essentials lay the foundation of your plan and will help you reach your goals. Here are some essentials you may wish to include:

State Your Purpose

- Why do you want to trade in the Forex market?

- What do you hope to gain from trading?

- What are your trading goals?

- How do you plan on becoming a better trader?

- How are you going to use your trading plan?

- Clearly define your purpose for trading and investing.

- State your goals and what you hope to gain and achieve through trading.

Strategy for Buying

- How are you going to find which pairs to trade? Examples: news, research, technical analysis, fundamental analysis, etc.

- How will you refine your "buy list" (currency pairs on your radar you are considering buying)?

- Using Technical Analysis: You need to understand what you are looking at. Understand how the indicators you use work and what they are measuring. Your favorite indicator may not be useful in many situations; in fact, I recommend using a number of indicators rather than just one. You must know when to use technicals and when not to use them.

- Using Fundamental Analysis: Fundamental News announcements can trigger the most volatile movements in this market. Make absolutely certain you understand how fundamentals work.

Strategy for Selling

- Set a desired minimum goal for each trade. You may be happy making 20 pips per trade, or 50 pips per trade. Set a goal you are happy with and stick to it.

- Use stop-loss orders to reduce risk by automatically selling at a pre-determined lowest price. Oddly enough this is a hotly debated subject. Before, I didn't trade with stops at all. Lately, the Euro and the Pound have taught me some hard lessons, and I will be incorporating stops into my strategy as I move forward.

- How much are you willing to lose if this trade goes bad?

- Some traders continually raise their stop-loss prices as the trade goes in their direction. This is called a trailing stop and can be a very useful tool for locking in gains and reducing risk.

Strategy for Holding

- What will you do if the price does not move at all after you buy? Sell it and move on, or hold it and wait for action?

- Some traders will hold on to the trade until more activity and volume pick up. They are comfortable waiting it out. This action may require more capital in your trading account, as you may have to hold on to more than one non-moving trade.

Money and Risk Management

- How will you keep your risks to a minimum?

- How will your keep your total account value at a maximum and grow it?

- Research money management techniques—there are many. This can include how much money or what percent of your entire portfolio value to use in each trade.

- Margin: margin can be a very useful tool for many traders, but can be scary and risky if not used properly. You can get a margin call from your broker at any time, which means they want to collect their money now. Margin gives you extra buying power. Margin also gives you additional risk. Use margin cautiously and wisely. Some traders do not use margin at all.

Like the Boy Scouts say, be prepared. Preparation for the Forex trader means making your plan, developing your strategies, testing your techniques, and continually refining it all. The process is never really over, and there are good trading opportunities to take advantage of out there. Having a well thought out plan is a solid foundation for a beginning trader. Be dedicated to your plan and stick to it. As I have said previously, I recommend trading on a demo account until you can show decent returns. Then begin to trade micro lots on a mini account. This will ensure that your plan is built upon sound principles and will benefit you in the long run.

How Much Should You Trade?

There are so many trading strategies out there and most of them work in given situations and not in others. There are forums, discussion groups, and an entire software industry that has grown up around the idea that the most important thing is the entry point. The fact is that the exit point and money management are more important than the entry. It is one thing to initiate a trade, and it is quite another to know when to get out and figure out how much you are willing to risk.

Think of it this way, let's place trades at random points on the chart (by the way, I don't advise this). We are assuming that this is truly random and likely to be about 50% potentially profitable trades and 50% unprofitable trades. If you used a 10 pip stop loss and a 20 pip take profit, then you would in fact make money because ½ of your trades would be positive for a larger number of your pips than you would lose. Now, realize that this is an extremely simplistic, naïve way to think about this and is more to illustrate a point. Not every trade will make a 20 pip gain without retracing to your stop loss. Your money management techniques will need to be a little more solidly thought out than my example.

Your Forex investment should only comprise about 10% of your risk capital. Remember, this is the riskiest form of investment in your portfolio, so don't dump your entire retirement fund into Forex. Also, don't look to Forex as a way of making a living if you have just been laid off. So, if you have $100,000 of risk capital (risk capital is money that you can afford to lose, not your retirement fund and definitely not your home), then you should feel free to invest $10,000 in the Forex market. However, if you are like many Americans and only have $10,000 or less in risk capital, then invest no more than $1,000 in this market.

The total amount that you should use to enter the market should be about 5% of the total equity in your account. If you are trading a $10,000 account, then don't use more than about $500 of your equity in the market (equal to about 5 mini lots). If your account is a $1,000 account, then you need to be careful trading more than a half of a mini lot at any one time. Now this may seem excessively conservative. Quite honestly, I have had a $500 mini account and have had four or five mini lots open at one time; but, this is completely over leveraged. Like many traders out there, I have felt the sting of the margin call. Slow and steady should be your credo. Remember, this is not a race. Be the turtle, not the rabbit.

What Are The Most Active Times To Trade?

It's funny, I talk to traders all over the world, and they are all under the impression that the best time to trade is two in the morning. If you think about it, two a.m. can't be the best time all over the world, can it? So when is the best time trade? The best times to trade in the Forex market are when there is more than one market open, hence higher volume and higher liquidity.

By taking a look at Figure 8.1, it is apparent that someone is selling currencies somewhere in the world at any given time during the week. As one market closes, another one opens. The market begins its week in New Zealand, followed by Australia, Asia, the Middle East, Europe, and then America. The U.S. and U.K. markets account for about half of all the market transactions, and nearly two-thirds of the New York trading activity occurs in the morning hours while the European markets are also open.

Forex market volume remains high during the entire day but trading is generally heaviest when the major markets overlap. Therefore, so the likelihood of a solid market move is highest during these periods.

What Pairs Should You Trade?

The most commonly traded currency pairs involve the U.S. dollar against another currency. The U.S. economy has traditionally been considered the largest in the world. The Japanese yen and the Swiss franc have also been the basis of a lot of trading as well. Each of these markets has very distinctive features.

FIGURE 8-1: WORLDWIDE TRADING SESSIONS

EST	1	2	3	4	5	6	7	8	9	10	11	12	13	14	15	16	17	18	19	20	21	22	23	24
London			■	■	■	■	■	■	■	■	■													
New York							■	■	■	■	■	■	■	■	■	■								
Sydney	■	■															■	■	■	■	■	■	■	■
Tokyo	■	■	■																■	■	■	■	■	■
Overlap								■	■	■	■													

THE 24 HOUR FOREX MARKET

65

US Dollar

The US dollar has suffered violent swings and the credibility of US economic policy has come under question numerous times. Following the Plaza accord the US dollar was dumped aggressively.

Japanese Yen

The yen has been volatile in recent years, strengthening during the nineties; however, in the past year or so, the problem of an appreciating exchange rate squeezing exports has encouraged the volatility.

The Swiss Franc

The independent and neutral political stance and secrecy of the Swiss banking system helps the Swissy serve as a safe haven. This combination has led to influxes into Swiss francs in times of insecurity and trouble.

How Do I Choose Take-Profit and Stop-Losses?

You have most likely identified a time frame that you are interested in trading and one or two currency pairs that you are committed to studying. Now it is time to identify what you want to make and what you are willing to lose per trade. Don't hold on to any illusions here; you will lose and you will lose regularly. The key is to lose well.

There are a number of theories surrounding take-profits and stop-losses. I believe that knowing when to exit a trade is nearly as important as know when to enter a trade, yet so much less attention is paid to it. I think this stems from the fact that it is a little subjective. It really depends on your time frame, your currency pair and what happens to your pair during your chosen time frame.

FIGURE 8-2: CURRENCY TRADING RANGES BY SESSION						
Currency Pairs	Asian Session	European Session	US Session	US & Europe Overlap	Europe & Asia Overlap
EST	7 pm – 4 am	2 am – 12 am	8 am – 5 pm	8 am – 12 pm	2 am – 4 am
EURUSD	51	87	78	65	32
USDJPY	78	79	69	58	29
GBPUSD	65	112	94	78	43
USDCHF	68	117	107	88	43
EURCHF	53	53	49	40	24
AUDUSD	38	53	47	39	20
USDCAD	47	94	84	74	28
NZDUSD	42	52	46	38	20
EURGBP	25	40	34	27	16
GBPJPY	112	145	119	99	60
GBPCHF	96	150	129	105	62
AUDJPY	55	63	56	47	26

I have put together Figure 8.2 as an example, but I would encourage you to build your own table every several months. The market does change over time; so don't get caught using old data in your analysis.

One quick caution before we delve in here: just because a pair has a huge trading range in a given session, it doesn't mean that it is the best pair to trade. The GBP/JPY has a huge trading range. It is an extremely volatile pair and has taken more than a few of my dollars.

The point I am trying to make here is that there are different ranges for different pairs across different time frames. For example, setting a 30 pip take profit on a AUD/USD trade placed during the Europe and Asia overlap would be sort of silly since the pair only has an average range of 20 pips during that time period.

Let's say your chosen trading system is correct 50% of the time. If your take-profits are usually 30 pips and your stop-losses are usually 15 pips, then you would be a profitable trader.

Another method for identifying stop losses is to use common indicators as exit strategies. One such indicator is the Parabolic SAR (see page 83 for additional details).

How Far Back Do You Look?

As you can imagine, it takes a lot of time and resources to look back too far on your charts. It is also commonly said that the market has a limited memory, meaning that looking too far back on charts is not really relevant. This holds some serious implications for volatile currency pairs and, particularly, for volatile market conditions. The basic premise is that you should only be looking at the last x number of candlesticks on your chart. The number x is determined by your time frame, the currency pair and the volatility. I have been to a number of seminars presented by all different experts, and they all have slightly different ideas on how this should work. I like to look at the last 100-ish candles on any given chart.

That is not to say I don't also look at multiple time frames when I am trading. I find it useful to look at the daily charts, and then look at progressively smaller time frames. While I look at the 15- and 30-minute charts, I personally like to trade off the one-hour charts.

As with all things trading related, these patterns should be used in conjunction with your favorite indicator, trend lines, support and resistance lines, or any of their various combinations. It is easy to get a single signal and jump on a trade without getting a confirmation from another source, which includes fundamental news announcements. There are hundreds of candlestick patterns that have been identified and documented. I think that learning to identify these particular patterns is a great first step in incorporating candlesticks into your trading style.

What Time Frames Should You be Looking At?

Well, that is completely up to you. It depends on your time commitments. It depends on your temperament. Can you go to sleep with an open trade? Are you going to be able to handle the market moving on you while you need to rest? If not, then you are better off making shorter-term trades and looking at 5-minute, 30-minute, or 1-hour charts. Are you patient? Can you wait? If not, again, you may be happier trading on the shorter time frame charts.

It also depends on your initial account size. A larger account will be able to handle the potential swings that can happen in longer- term trading.

What Should My Daily Goal Be In Profit or Losses?

This is an interesting question. The first answer you are likely to give is that you only want profits and no losses at all. Well, unfortunately, that is not always possible; and, if you commit to zero losses, you automatically set yourself up to fail and will end up doing bad things to your head when you do take a loss. You will also want to make your daily profit goals reasonable: No need to create stress with unachievable goals.

When you are choosing your daily profit and loss goals you need to consider the power of compounding capital.

For instance, the first month you need to make $100 trading .1 lots. That equates to about 50 pips a day. If there were 20 trading days in that particular month, 50 pips a day is achievable. But I also consider it a little high, depending on your pair and time frame.

The other wrench I would like to toss at this monkey is that most platforms and brokers will only allow you to trade a max number of lots at one time—like 50. So somewhere in your third year, you are going to have to open multiple positions at once to try to achieve that 50 pip gain. I also think that by following this "system" you are not considering losses, and you are over leveraging your account.

So, be realistic about your goals, and I think you will be pleasantly surprised. I don't think it is any surprise that the most successful (long term) traders I know are the ones that have been in the market for years.

Being Out of the Market Can Be a Good Move

As you are putting together your trading plan, you need to give yourself some breathing space. If you set the pace too briskly, you may end up burning out or having to rewrite your plan not long after you begin to trade. Being out of the market can be good for a number of reasons. One reason is that you still have a life to lead. Take me, for example:

- I work a full time job.
- I have a young child.
- I am remodeling my house.
- I still like to visit with my friends and family.

That doesn't leave a whole lot of room for trading. I like to spend an hour or so checking out my charts every day, but some days I am just spent. I don't want to trade, and I certainly don't want to add one more thing to my schedule. Some days, you are just not going to want to trade.

Also, take a vacation. Earlier this year I spent a week in Maui recharging my batteries. I actually brought the cell phone, the PDA, a laptop, and three novels thinking that I would sit on the beach or balcony sipping a Mai Tai and work. The reality is that I opened my computer once every couple of days and didn't do much else. All right, I am lying. The cell phone was still surgically attached but even that is a huge step for me. I didn't work. I didn't trade. I didn't watch the news. I took a break and I came back with a much better perspective on my trading and life.

If you build in time to be out of the market and end up trading by choice, you will be ahead of the game. If you take the necessary sanity break, then you will still be happily on course.

How Long Should You Use a Demo Account Before You Go Live?

This is a hard question and completely up to you. This will depend on what kind of strategy you put together. Remember, you should be playing with a demo account as you are putting together your strategy. If you have a fairly good idea of what and when you are going to trade and what your expectations are, your demo trading should fall into line fairly quickly. If your expectations are way out of line, then you will struggle with a demo.

The other reason you may struggle with a demo account is if you don't have a clearly defined path. You may be just randomly picking trades off many different charts. If you are doing this, you are not becoming acquainted with your pair and learning its idiosyncrasies. You are actually making trading harder than it needs to be.

Once you can consistently make gains in your demo account that are equal to those that you expect, then, and only then, should you switch to a live account. There is no urgency to switch. Anyone who tells you otherwise has an agenda. The market has been here for years and will continue to be here. Take your time and make the right decisions for you.

How is a Demo Different Than a Live Account?

The best, and only, answer to this question is Y-O-U. Once you put real money in the market, the game really changes. Even if it is a $250 mini-account and you are trading .01 lots (which I recommend), your perspective will change when real money is on the line. For whatever reason, your gains will elate you and the losses will be devastating. You will find you are taking risks with your losses (letting them ride, rather than pulling out like you know you should) and being miserly with the gains.

I would recommend you make a conscious effort to be brutal with your losses and take a little more liberty with your gains. As the pair moves in your direction, why not move your stop loss up as well, but let it run further if it has the momentum. Set a trailing stop if your broker offers one, or you can manually move your stop-loss up as the pair moves in your direction. Wouldn't it please you if you made 30 pips out of a 50 pip move rather than a 20 pip gain? Don't be greedy and say, "No, I would have rather made 50." No one buys at the low and sells at the high. And if they tell you they do, then they most likely have a bit of swampland for you as well.

Check the Crosses and Relative Pairs

This is an interesting phenomenon. Currency pairs often move in correlation with each other, either in the same direction or the exact opposite. Examples of pairs that tend to have a strong negative correlation are the EUR/USD and the USD/CHF. An example of a pair that has a strong positive correlation with each other is the GBP/JPY and the EUR/JPY. Check the charts and watch for another pair that has a strong relationship to your chosen pair. These can server either as a leading indicator or a confirmation depending on the relationship between the pairs.

Remember that these trends do not hold water all the time. Watch these in correlation with your other indicators. There is a fairly well known strategy that uses pairs that have an inverse relationship, one of which earns a fair amount in swap, the other that pays a smaller amount in swap. The theory is that the trades will serve as a hedge for each other, and the trader will earn the swap. While this is an interesting strategy, and there are many that have success stories trading this way, be aware that I have also seen this particular strategy lose customers substantial amounts of money. Do not get over confident and over leverage yourself; you are not truly hedged.

The charts on the following pages will show currency pairs that have correlating and inverse relationships.

Currency pairs that tend to have a correlating relationship (Figure 8.3):

EUR/USD and GBP/USD

EUR/USD and NZD/USD

USD/CHF and USD/JPY

AUD/USD and GBP/USD

AUD/USD and EUR/USD

Currency pairs that tend to have an inverse relationship (Figure 8.4):

EUR/USD and USD/CHF

GBP/USD and USD/JPY

GBP/USD and USD/CHF

AUD/USD and USD/CAD

AUD/USD and USD/JPY

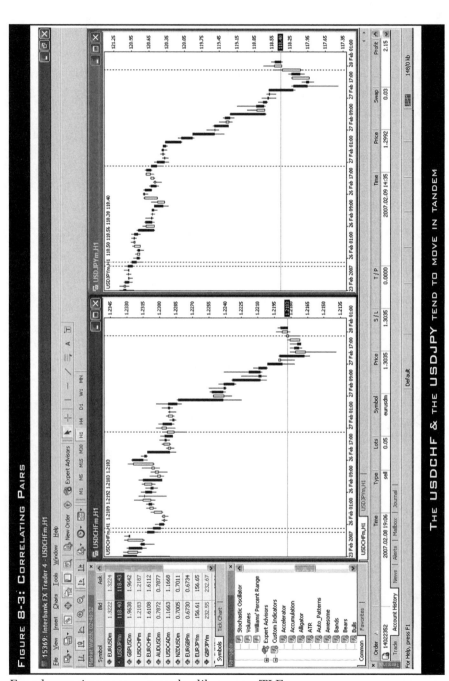

FIGURE 8-3: CORRELATING PAIRS

THE USDCHF & THE USDJPY TEND TO MOVE IN TANDEM

For a larger view go to www.traderslibrary.com/TLEcorner

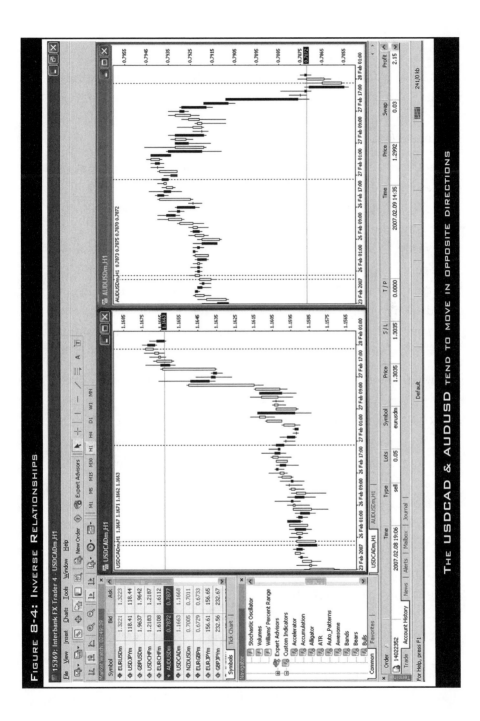

FIGURE 8-4: INVERSE RELATIONSHIPS

THE USDCAD & AUDUSD TEND TO MOVE IN OPPOSITE DIRECTIONS

Getting Stopped Out on a Chart

This is a very important point. I hear about this issue from new traders in the Forex market whether they have been around other markets or not. There are some pretty stubborn myths in relation to this issue, and it is important that you pay attention here.

A common theme that you will hear repeated across cyber space is, "My broker cheated me… I was taken out of a trade and my price was never hit." Well, first of all, if you blow up your account and fade into trading obscurity, who wins? Is it you? Well, of course not. Is it your broker? Not really. If you blow up your account and stop trading, your broker isn't going to be all that pleased. They would like a customer for life, or at least a few more years. The answer is that the market is king. In other words, some guy in another country made the opposite trade from you and made a bit of money, or a corporation got in to cover some contracts or payroll contracts.

So, what happened on your chart? Well the long and the short of it is that a chart in the Forex world can be misleading. That is because the EUR/USD (or whatever pair you choose) has two prices, the bid and the ask. So, in reality, your chart should look like it has a shadow on it. Let's assume you go short on the EUR/USD and set your stop-loss at 1.2575. You are watching your charts and watching your charts and… the chart hits 1.2573! Bingo, your stop-loss kicks in and takes you out of the trade. Of course the chart immediately turns around and heads back the other way and you miss out on a terrific trade.

You fume and you swear and you holler, "How dare your broker do this to you?" But the truth of the matter is that if the spread at that time was 2 pips, the ask price was actually 1.2573 and the stop was valid. If your broker employs a fixed pip spread policy (or in other words, if they are a market maker), then this is fairly easy to anticipate and make accommodations for. However, if your broker employs a straight-through processing methodology, it is highly likely that the spreads will fluctuate, making the management of these stops, take-profits, and buy-limit orders harder. Being aware of what you are looking at puts you ahead of the game.

The USD/CAD chart in Figure 8.5 has the ask line highlighted. You can see the bid price in the candle. The difference between the two is 5 pips, reflecting the spread. Setting stop-losses and take-profits without analyzing the spread is a surefire recipe for frustration.

Trading Like a Girl

I loved this title when my husband used it in an article, so I had to steal it. It is true that I have been known to buy the pair (or more) of shoes when the prices drop. Even though I don't really need them and sometimes don't end up liking them. There is some power in the word SALE.

In most trading circles this is called "pyramiding", usually said with a heaping of scorn slathered on top. Pyramiding can mean many different things and is something I don't want to debate here, so I will continue to call my method "trading like a girl."

The last time I traded like a girl, it worked like this: I woke up early and saw the EUR/USD on sale (trading at what I considered to be a low price), so I bought a lot. I went to work, attended a few meetings, got back to my desk, and checked the EUR/USD. It had moved against me, but all I saw was the EUR/USD on sale at an even bigger discount, so I bought again. I finished my day, went home, sorted out dinner, and checked my charts again. Both trades were now against me but again, all I saw was the EUR/USD on sale at an even bigger discount again. So… I bought again.

Ridiculous behavior, wasn't it? But I wasn't focusing on my plan, or the market. All I was seeing was a bright red SALE sign. That influenced my trading. It took me a while to dig out of that hole.

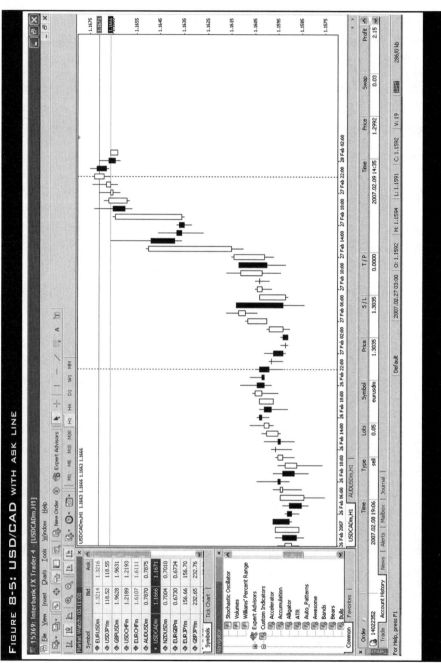

FIGURE 8-5: USD/CAD WITH ASK LINE

For a larger view go to www.traderslibrary.com/TLEcorner

Conclusion

So, still looking to the Forex market to spice up your life? Well, I know how you feel. The currency market is the only market that I actively trade in these days. I hope you have learned to think for yourself, make your own decisions, and formulate your own plan. If I see you at the next Traders expo, I expect you to swing by and say hello. I also expect to see you carefully analyzing the products on offer. You now have the knowledge that you need to decide what, when, and how you are going to trade. You don't need some slick-suited salesperson to sell you on the green and red arrows.

Welcome to the beauty and the madness that is this market. Remember (please) that this game should only be played with the money you can easily afford to lose. If you tell me you have mortgaged the house, or taken out $30k on interest free credit cards, I am going to be angry. Start the same as the rest of us crazies… with a free demo, then graduate to a mini account and trade pennies. You will thank me when you are only down 50 cents rather than 50 percent of your account. And best of all, enjoy yourself.

See you around the water cooler!

Appendix A:
Common Indicators Defined

Bollinger Bands

Created by and named for John Bollinger, Bollinger Bands are plotted at standard deviation levels above and below a moving average (Figure A.1). Since standard deviation is a measure of volatility, the bands will

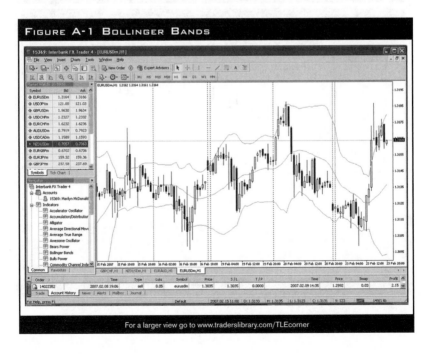

FIGURE A-1 BOLLINGER BANDS

For a larger view go to www.traderslibrary.com/TLEcorner

81

widen during volatile markets and contract during more settled periods. What you see on your charts is essentially three lines displayed in a band.

The bands are at their widest when the prices are volatile, and narrow when the prices enter a consolidation period. The narrowing of the bands increases the probability of a breakout. Prices are considered overbought on the upside of the band and oversold on the bottom side of the bands. The simplest way to use this indicator is to use the upper and lower bands as price targets.

Standard Deviation

Standard Deviation is a volatility indicator. The highvales occur when the price is swinging dramatically, and low values occur when the price is stable (Figure A.2).

FIGURE A-2 STANDARD DEVIATION

For a larger view go to www.traderslibrary.com/TLEcorner

Moving Average Convergence/ Divergence (MACD)

The MACD is well known and widespread. It shows the relationship between two moving averages of prices. The MACD is the difference between a 26-day and a 12-day exponential moving average. A 9-day exponential moving average is plotted on top of the MACD to act as a signal line (Figure A.3).

The most common interpretation of this indicator is to watch the cross-overs. The general idea is to sell when the MACD falls below the signal line and then to buy when the MACD rises above the signal line.

Parabolic SAR

The Parabolic Time/Price System (Parabolic SAR – Stop and Reversal) is generally used to help identify trailing price stops. It was originally

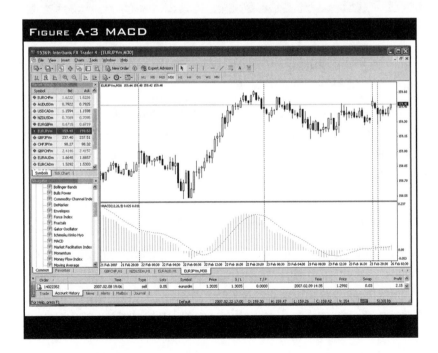

FIGURE A-3 MACD

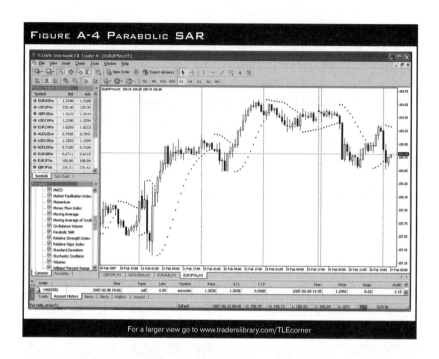

For a larger view go to www.traderslibrary.com/TLEcorner

defined by Welles Wilder and is defined in detail in Wilder's book, *New Concepts in Technical Trading Systems.*

It is used to define exit points (Figure A-4). The generally accepted interpretation is to close your long positions when the SAR indicator appears above the price bars and close short positions when the SAR indicator appears below the price bars.

Double Exponential Moving Average (DEMA)

The DEMA is a composite of a single exponential moving average and a double exponential moving average. It was developed by Patrick Mulloy and first presented in the January 1994 issues of *Technical Analysis of Stocks and Commodities.* It is a unique calculation that is not simply an exponential moving average. The indicator provides less lag time than

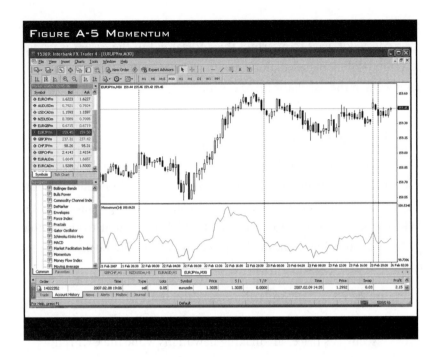

FIGURE A-5 MOMENTUM

either of its components. You can use the DEMA rather than your ordinary exponential moving average, or you can use it to smooth your price data.

Triple Exponential Moving Average (TEMA)

The TEMA is composed of a single exponential moving average, a double exponential moving average, and a triple exponential moving average. Developed by Patrick Mulloy, the TEMA is really an extension of the DEMA and can be used in place of an exponential moving average.

Momentum

The Momentum indicator measures the amount that a security's price has changed over a given time span (Figure A.5).

The Momentum indicator displays the rate of change as a ratio. There are a couple of ways to interpret this indicator, but the easiest is using it as a trend-following oscillator—buying when the indicator turns up and selling when the oscillator turns down.

Commodity Channel Index

The Commodity Channel Index (CCI) is said to measure the variation of a security's price from its statistical mean. Or, in plain English, whether the security is overbought or oversold (Figure A.6). High values indicate that prices are deemed to be unusually high compared to the average price, and low values indicate that prices are deemed to be unusually low compared to the average price.

There are two basic methods of interpreting the CCI:

• Looking for a divergence. A divergence occurs when the security's prices are making new highs while the CCI is not

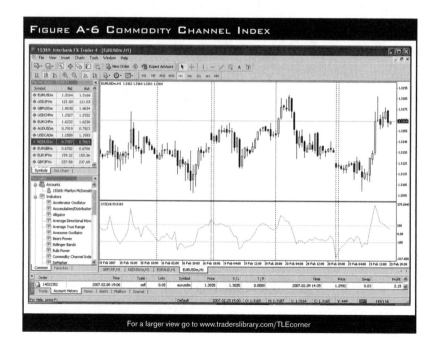

FIGURE A-6 COMMODITY CHANNEL INDEX

For a larger view go to www.traderslibrary.com/TLEcorner

passing its previous highs. A divergence may be followed by a correction in the security's price.

- Using the CCI as an overbought/oversold indicator. Readings above 100 indicate an overbought situation and a possible price correction, while readings below 100 indicate an oversold situation and a possible price rally. Most traders use the CCI in this way.

Relative Strength Index (RSI)

The Relative Strength Index (RSI) is an oscillator that was identified by Welles Wilder. The RSI attempts to measure the strength of the security. The original RSI was a 14-day RSI, though many now use the 9-day and the 25-day RSI. The RSI compares the relative strength of price advances to price declines over a specific period (Figure A.7).

FIGURE A-7 RSI

The RSI ranges between 0 and 100. The most popular way of interpreting this indicator is to look for a divergence. For example, look for when the security's price is reaching a new high but the RSI fails to surpass a previous high. The divergence is an indication that the price may reverse. When the RSI turns and falls down to a new low, it is called a "Failure Swing." That is said to be a confirmation of the indicated reversal. Most traders agree that Failure Swings, when the RSI is over 70 or under 30, are the ones to look for.

Stochastic Oscillator

The Stochastic Oscillator is displayed as two lines. The solid line is called a %K. The dotted line is called %D and is a moving average of the %K (Figure A.8).

FIGURE A-8 STOCHASTICS

For a larger view go to www.traderslibrary.com/TLEcorner

There are a couple of different ways to interpret this indicator. You can buy when either line is below 20 and then rises above, and then sell when either line is above 80 and then falls below. You can buy when the solid line rises above the dotted line, and then sell when the solid line falls below the dotted line. Or, you can look for divergences. For example, look for when the price is reaching new highs but the indicator is not reaching its previous highs.

Fibonacci Line Studies

Indicators and line studies seem to have seasons. At some stage or another you will come across Fibonacci season. Leonardo Fibonacci was a mathematician who was born in Italy in about 1170. Fibonacci numbers are a sequence of numbers in which each successive number is the sum of the two previous numbers:

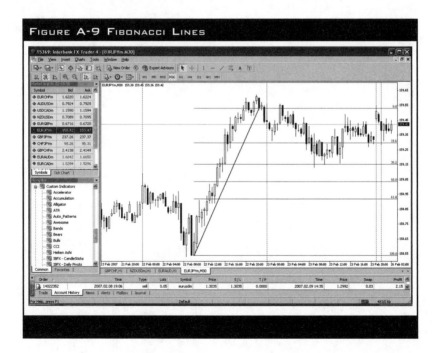

FIGURE A-9 FIBONACCI LINES

1, 1, 2, 3, 5, 8, 13, 21, 34, 55, 89, 144, 233, 377, and so on…

There are four common Fibonacci studies that you are likely to come across: arcs, fans, retracements, and time zones. The most popular is the Fibonacci Retracements (Figure A.9).

To apply the Fibonacci retracement, you should first draw a trend line between two points on your chart (a lower low and a higher high), then apply your Fibonacci retracement on top of your trend line. This will create six lines on your chart at the 0.0% level, the 23.6% level, the 38.2% level, the 50.0% level, the 61.8% level, and the 100% level. Many traders believe that after a significant price move (either up or down), prices will often retrace a portion, if not all, of the original move. As prices retrace, support and resistance levels will often occur at or near the Fibonacci Retracement levels.

APPENDIX B:
Trend Line Work Book

Break out your pencil and your ruler, and draw some trend lines. You will be right some times and wrong others. Don't worry about it. Just see if you can identify the trend.

For charts with the correct trend lines go to www.traderslibrary.com/TLEcorner.

FIGURE B.1 NZD/USD

1 HOUR 4/16/2007
For a larger view go to www.traderslibrary.com/TLEcorner

91

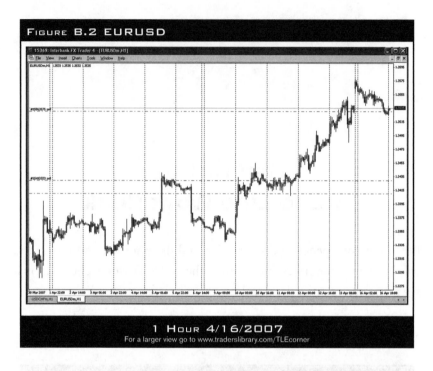

Figure B.2 EURUSD

1 Hour 4/16/2007
For a larger view go to www.traderslibrary.com/TLEcorner

Figure B.3 EURUSD

1 Hour 4/17/2007

FIGURE B.4 EURUSD

1 HOUR 4/16/2007

FIGURE B.5 USDCHF

1 HOUR 4/17/2007

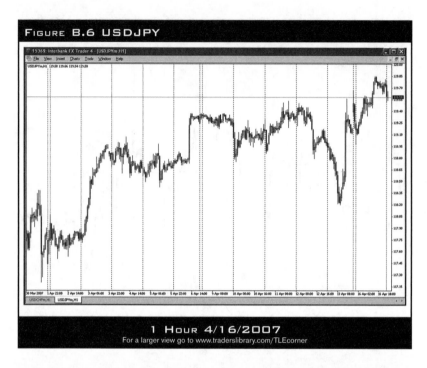

Figure B.6 USDJPY

1 Hour 4/16/2007

For a larger view go to www.traderslibrary.com/TLEcorner

Figure B.7 USDJPY

1 Hour 4/17/2007

Appendix C:
Finding Patterns in Your Charts

Chart patterns have been around forever. They are very well document-ed by a number of experts. I am probably not going to be covering any ground breaking ground here, but it is well worth noting chart patterns and looking for them while you are trading. They can be remarkably accurate, though I couldn't say whether that is due to the patterns them-selves or the psychology of the people watching the patterns. If you find a pattern that you are interested in, I would recommend doing an Inter-net search or finding a book that breaks down chart patterns in detail.

Double Top (Reversal)—This is a pattern that describes the rise of a stock's price, a drop, a rise to the same level, and yet another drop. It resembles the letter M on a chart.

Double Bottom (Reversal)—The opposite of a double bottom, this is a pattern that begins with the drop of a stock's price, a rise, a drop to the same level, and yet another rise. It resembles the letter W on a chart.

Head and Shoulders Top (Reversal)—This is a major reversal pattern, but it has some caveats. There needs to be an existing uptrend and there should be three well-defined peaks. The head should be slightly higher than the shoulders. One thing to remember is that the pattern is not complete until the resulting price has broken down below the neckline.

Head and Shoulders Bottom (Reversal)—This is also called an inverse head and shoulders. It is pretty much the opposite of the Head and Shoulders Top. There is quite a lot of discussion in both the Head and Shoulders Top and Bottom patterns surrounding the importance of volume, particularly among those chartists that trade securities other than Forex. Remember, in Forex there is no valid volume measurement. Your broker may give volume data, but that is likely tick volume and pretty useless in any practical application.

Triple Top and Triple Bottom (Reversal)—This pattern is a variation of the Head and Shoulders Top and Head and Shoulders Bottom, albeit a little more rare. This pattern starts out as a Head and Shoulders Top (or Bottom) but, at some stage, the prices resume their initial trend. This is a tricky little pattern that simply highlights the need for the technical trader to be watching his/her charts for signs that their initial analysis is wrong. Also, a point of interest is that once a breakout occurs, a retracement back to the breakout point is not unusual.

Flag, Pennant (Continuation)—The difference between a flag and a pennant is that the pennant pattern looks like a pennant because it has lower highs and higher lows. These patterns are quite common and represent a pause in a market move. They are usually preceded by a sharp market move and represent great continuation patterns. Flags and pennants are considered to fly at half-mast on the flagpole. The flagpole will be the sharp move just prior to the consolidation.

Symmetrical Triangle (Continuation)—The Symmetrical Triangle is usually a continuation pattern. It signifies a pause in the existing trend and after which the existing trend resumes.

Ascending Triangle (Continuation)—The Ascending Triangle has a horizontal resistance area that gets tested repeatedly. Moves down from this resistance line are progressively higher lows. This shows that even though there is resistance, demand is getting progressively more aggressive.

Descending Triangle (Continuation)—The Descending Triangle is a pattern where the horizontal resistance area serves as support. Moves up from this support line are progressively lower highs.

Rectangle (Continuation)—This pattern is known by many names. It is a sideways movement in the price bars on the chart that moves between two parallel lines, sort of like a channel that moves horizontally.

Price Channel (Continuation)—The price channel, or channel line, is essentially a variation of the trend line. You will essentially draw the basic trend line along the lows and then draw a second trend line along the highs. The bottom trend line can be used for entry signals (long positions, of course). It is important to watch both lines on your channel however, as a failure to reach the top trend line could signal weakness, and you should watch for a reversal in the market.

Measured Move Bullish & Bearish (Continuation)—The Measured Move describes an event where a major market move is split into two equal parts. The theory is that the second part of the advance is similar to the size and slope of the first advance with a correction in the middle that often retraces about 1/3 of the initial advance.

Cup and Handle (Continuation)—A pattern that resembles a cup with a handle. It shows how a price can move sideways, and go into a downtrend for weeks at a time, and then take off.

Candlestick Patterns

A Quick History

The Japanese began using candlesticks and technical analysis to trade rice in the 17th century. Much of the credit for the development of candlesticks is attributed to a legendary rice trader named Homma from the town of Sakata. He reportedly amassed a great fortune trading in the rice market. This early version is markedly different from the candlesticks that we know and love today, but many of the underlying principles are the same.

There have been countless books and articles written about candlesticks, and most traders have used them and prefer candlestick charts over any other. One of the predominant experts in the field of candlesticks is Steve Nison. If you are hungry for more information, I would suggest picking up one of his books; they are a great starting point.

As is the case with all styles of analysis, there are observable recurring patterns on the candlestick charts. These patterns are very good visual representation of the price movements and can give traders a good grasp of what is going on in the market.

What is a Candlestick?

Candlesticks are drawn with the same open, high, low, and close information as bar charts. The rectangular middle section of the candle is called the real body. The real body represents the open and the close. If the real body is black (or filled in), it means that session was bearish, or the close was lower than the open. If the real body is white (or hollow), it means the session was bullish, or the open was lower than the close. The lines on the top and the bottom of the real body are called shadows. The shadow represents the trading range during the session. If the candle has no upper shadow, it has a shaven head. If the candle has no lower shadow, then it has a shaven bottom.

One of the nice things about candlestick charts is that they can give you clues that you cannot get on bar charts.

The Patterns

There are, quite literally, hundreds of different patterns, some signal bearish or bullish reversals, some trend continuation. Each pattern can be categorized by reliability in a given market. I am choosing only to discuss patterns I consider to be reliable. For example a "Three Outside Up" pattern is a confirmed "Bullish Engulfing". I consider the former pattern to be more reliable than the latter mainly because it is less common than say a hammer pattern. The definitions and calculations of candlesticks are no mystery, so I am not unleashing any secrets here. However, these are the patterns I feel add the most value to my trading.

Morning Star or Morning Doji Star

Some of the most talked about reversal patterns fall into the star family. A star is a small real body that gaps away from the previous candle's large real body. In the cases when the open is equal to the close, you have what is called a doji pattern. The Morning Doji Star is a three-candlestick formation that signals a major bottom. The name is derived from the planet Mercury (the morning star) that foretells the sunrise; it signals higher prices. It is composed of a first long black body, a second small real body, white or black, gapping lower to form a star. These two candlesticks define a basic star pattern. The third is a white candlestick that closes well into the first session's black real body. The third candlestick shows that the market is now turning bullish.

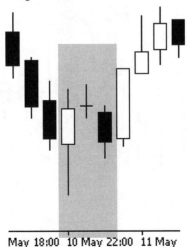

May 18:00 10 May 22:00 11 May

99

Evening Star or Evening Doji Star

The Evening Doji Star is the bearish counterpart of the Morning Doji Star. It is named after the planet Venus that appears just before darkness. This is a major top reversal pattern formed by three candlesticks. The first candlestick is a long white body; the second one is a small real body that may be white. It is characteristically marked with a gap in a higher direction thus forming a star. In fact, the first two candlesticks form a basic star pattern. Finally, we see the black candlestick with a closing price well within the first session's white real body. This pattern indicates that the market has now turned bearish.

Since the Evening Doji Star is a top reversal pattern, it should really only be considered if it shows up after an uptrend.

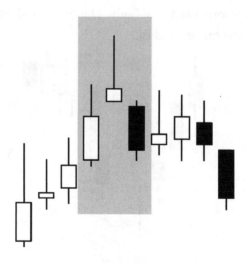

For color charts go to www.traderslibrary.com/TLEcorner

Three White Soldiers

The Bullish Three White Soldiers Pattern is indicative of a strong reversal in the market. It is characterized by three long candlesticks stepping upward like a staircase. The opening of each day is slightly lower than a previous close, rallying then to a short term high. I would recommend only using this pattern if candles are gradual and steady. If the candles show signs of weakening, then you should be careful. Likewise, if the candles are very extended you should be wary of the market being overbought.

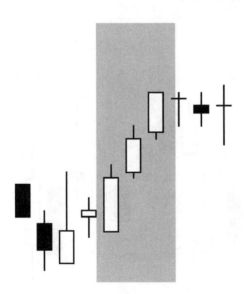

Three Black Crows

Three declining consecutive candles are called Three Black Crows. This pattern suggests a strong reversal during an uptrend. It consists of three long black candlesticks, which looks like a stair stepping downward. The opening price of each day is higher than the previous day's closing price, suggesting a move to a new short term low. Three Black Crows suggest lower prices if they appear at high price levels or after a strong advance.

This pattern is useful for longer-term traders since the pattern is not complete for three candles.

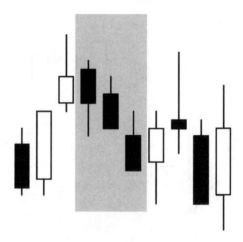

For color charts go to www.traderslibrary.com/TLEcorner

Three Inside Up

The Bullish Three Inside Up Pattern is another name for the Confirmed Bullish Harami Pattern. The third day is confirmation of the bullish trend reversal.

Three Inside Down

The Bearish Three Inside Down Pattern is also known as the Confirmed Bearish Harami Pattern. The third day confirms the bearish trend reversal.

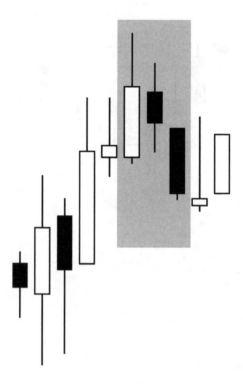

For color charts go to www.traderslibrary.com/TLEcorner

Three Outside Up

The Bullish Three Outside Up Pattern is simply another name for the Confirmed Bullish Engulfing Pattern. The third day is confirmation of the bullish trend reversal.

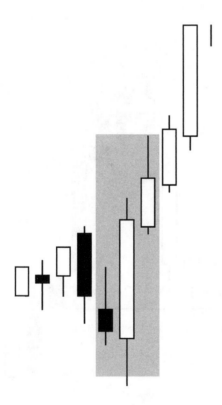

Three Outside Down

The Bearish Three Outside Down Pattern is another name for the Con-firmed Bearish Engulfing Pattern. The third day confirms the bearish trend reversal.

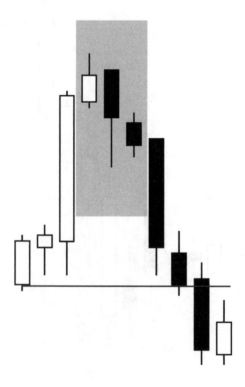

For color charts go to www.traderslibrary.com/TLEcorner

Piercing Line

Bullish Piercing Line Pattern is a bottom reversal pattern. The piercing pattern is composed of two candles in a falling market. A long black candlestick is followed by a gap lower during the next day while the market is in downtrend. The day ends up as a strong white candlestick, which closes more than halfway into the prior black candlestick's real body.

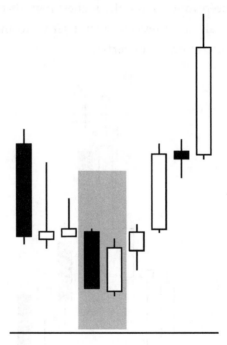

Dark Cloud Cover

The Dark Cloud Cover pattern is considered a reversal pattern. It is a two-candlestick pattern signaling a top reversal after an uptrend or, at times, at the top of a congestion band. We see a strong white real body in the first day. The second day opens strongly above the previous day's high (it is above the top of the upper shadow). However, the market closes near the low of the day and well within the prior day's white body at the end of the day. The greater the degree of penetration into the real white body, the more likely it is that this is a top.

Something to keep your eye on: the highest high that formed the dark cloud cover can also be a resistance level. It is worth noting the Dark Cloud Cover patterns on your charts.

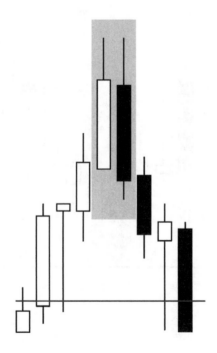

For color charts go to www.traderslibrary.com/TLEcorner

Appendix D:
More News to Trade

The Business Cycle

Economic indicators are often classified according to how they are related to the business cycle. If they:

- reflect the currency state of the economy, they are coincident.

- predict a future condition, they are leading.

- confirm that a turning occurred, they are lagging.

The organization responsible for an indicator generally distributes its reports about an hour before the official release time to financial news outlets (Reuters, CNBC, Dow Jones Newswires, Bloomberg, etc.). The reporters, who are literally locked in a room and not permitted to have contact with anyone outside, ask questions of the agency officials and prepare the headlines and analysis of the report contents. These stories are embargoed until the official release time, at which time they are transmitted over the newswires to be picked over by the Wall Street community and the traders that rely on them. Most Wall Street firms employ economists to provide live broadcasts of the numbers as they run across the newswires, together with interpretation and commentary regarding likely market reaction. This is known as the "hoot and the holler" or tape reading. The more that an indicator deviates from Wall Street expectations, the greater its effect on the financial markets.

Gross Domestic Product GDP

The GDP is a combination of economics and accounting. It is the broadest, most comprehensive barometer of a country's overall economic condition. It is quite literally the sum of all the market values of all final goods and services produced in a country (domestically) during a specific period using that country's resources, regardless of the ownership of the resources.

The U.S. GDP is calculated and reported on a quarterly basis as part of the National Income and Product Accounts (NIPAs). NIPAs were developed and are maintained today by the Commerce Department's Bureau of Economic Analysis (BEA). NIPAs are the most comprehensive set of data available regarding US national output, production, and the distribution of income. Each GDP report contains data on the following:

- personal income and consumption expenditures
- corporate profits
- national income
- inflation

To calculate GDP, the BEA uses the aggregate expenditure equation:

$$GDP = C + I + G + (X - M)$$

C = Personal Consumption Expenditures. It is the total market value of household purchases during the accounting term, including items such as beer, telephone service, golf clubs, CDs, gasoline, musical instruments, and taxicab rides.

I = Gross Private Domestic Investment. It is spending by businesses, expenditures on residential housing and apartments, and inventories. Inventories are valued by the BEA at the prevailing market price.

G = Government consumption expenditures and gross investment. It covers all money laid out by federal, state, and local governments for goods and services.

(X – M) = Net Exports of goods and services. It is the difference between the dollar value of the goods and services sent abroad and those it takes in across its borders.

The GDP report is a mother lode of information about a nation's economy. One commonly used trading strategy is calculating the output gap of the GDP. The output gap is the difference between the economy's actual and potential levels of production. This difference yields insight into important economic conditions, such as employment and inflation.

The economy's potential output is the amount of goods and services it would produce if it utilized all its resources. Economists estimate the rate at which the economy can expand without sparking a rise in inflation. It is not an easy calculation, and it yields as many different answers as the economists who calculate it. Luckily, a widely accepted estimate of potential output is reported relatively frequently by the Congressional Budget Office (www.cbo.gov). This website has information about methodology, underlying assumptions in computing the trend level, and detailed historical data.

Indices of Leading, Lagging and Coincident Indicators

This report is compiled by the Conference Board and published in its monthly Business Cycle Indicators report. It is released to the public at 10:00 a.m. (EST), four to five weeks after the end of the record month. You can visit www.conference-board.org for historical data and explanations of the methodology behind the indices. The market generally doesn't react strongly to this report because the indices' components are all released earlier than the indices themselves.

Coincident Index—The four components of this index are the number of employees on nonagricultural payroll (Non-Farm), personal income less transfer payments, industrial production index, and manufacturing and retail trade sales. Non-Farm payroll is obtained from a survey of about 160,000 businesses, conducted by the Bureau of Labor Statistics.

Personal Income Less Transfer Payments—This is derived from the Personal Income and Outlays report, produced by the Bureau of Economic Analysis (BEA). The largest source is wages and salaries, transfer payments, government disbursements, and food stamps

Total Industrial Production Index—This index is published by the Federal Reserve and is constructed of 295 components that are weighted according to the value they add during the production process.

Manufacturing and Retail Trade Sales—This is collected as part of the National Income and Product Accounts calculations. It is found in the Manufacturing and Trade Inventories and Sales (MTIS) report published by the Department of Commerce.

Leading Economic Index—The ten components of this index include average weekly hours worked in manufacturing, average weekly initial claims for unemployment insurance, manufacturers' new orders for consumer goods and materials, and 500 common stocks.

The individual indicators composing the Leading Economic Index differ considerably in their abilities to predict economic turning points. Some are very far seeing, others relatively near-sighted. The composite index is combined in such a way that the whole is designed to outperform any of its parts.

Lagging Economic Index—The seven components include average duration of unemployment, the ratio of manufacturing and trade inventories to sales, manufacturing labor cost per unit of output, and the average prime rate.

The Lagging Economic Index follows downturns in the business cycles by about three months and expansions by about fifteen. This index was designed to confirm turning points in economic activity that were identified by the leading and coincident indices that have actually occurred, thus preventing the transmission of false signals.

The Employment Situation

The most important U.S. economic indicator by far is the monthly Employment Situation published by the Bureau of Labor Statistics (BLS). No other report has the potential to move the Forex market like employment, and no other indicator is more revealing of general economic conditions than the labor market data. Employment data is important because it reveals how firms, corporations, and others responsible for hiring decisions view the current and upcoming economic environment.

The monthly employment report is based on two separate surveys: 1) the Current Population Survey (CPS), also known as the household survey; and 2) the Current Employment Statistics Survey (CES), also known as the establishment, or payrolls survey. Supplemental to each release, the commissioner of the Bureau of Labor Statistics provides a statement to the Joint Economic Committee of the U.S. Congress. The statement, generally three pages long, highlights significant strengths and weaknesses in the monthly employment statistics.

Top billing on the employment report is generally shared by two figures: the unemployment rate and the monthly change in Non-Farm payrolls. Average hourly earnings, hours worked, overtime hours worked, and the monthly change in manufacturing jobs also command a great deal of traders' attention.

In the employment surveys, the BLS includes only persons older than 16. Excluded from surveys are people in mental or penal institutions and members of the armed forces. People qualify as employed in two ways. First are those who, during a given period, have worked as paid employees in someone else's company or in their own businesses, own their own farms, or have done fifteen hours or more of unpaid labor in a family-operated enterprise. Second are those with jobs or in businesses from which they have take temporary leave, paid or unpaid, because of illness, bad weather, vacation, child-care problems, labor disputes, maternity or paternity leave, or other family or personal obligations.

Unemployed people are those not working during the period in question, whether they voluntarily terminated their employment, in which case they are classified as job leavers, or they were involuntarily laid off, making them job losers.

Strong relationships exist between the employment data and virtually every other indicator. The growth rate of Non-Farm payrolls is generally strongly correlated with the growth rate of GDP, industrial production and capacity utilization, consumer confidence, spending, and income.

Industrial Production and Capacity Utilization

The Industrial Production and Capacity Utilization report is assembled and released around the fifteenth of each month by the Board of Governors of the Federal Reserve System. It presents the data on the output of the nation's manufacturing, mining, and utility sectors. Also known as the Federal Reserve's G17 report, it organizes this data into industrial production and capacity utilization indices. The former measures the physical volume of the output of various industries and markets; the later shows what portion of the nation's production capacity was involved in creating that output. The Industrial Production and Capacity Utilization release, along with the historical data, is available on the Federal Reserve's website, www.federalreserve.gov.

The Industrial Production and Capacity Utilization report is an assemblage of 15 tables arranged over 19 or 20 pages. They display the current month's values for the various industrial-production and capacity-utilization indices, revisions to the previous months' values, month-to-month percentage changes in the indices, and their quarterly and annual rates of growth.

The industrial production indices measure quantity of output, not dollar volume, relative to a base year, currently 1997, whose value is set at 100. The Federal Reserve obtains the production data it uses to construct these indices both directly and indirectly. Direct sources include trade associations such as the American Forest and Paper Association, the U.S. Geological Survey, the Internal Revenue Service, and the Tanner's Council of America. Actual production data, however, is available at different times for different industries. When hard figures aren't available, the Federal Reserve estimates output based on the number of production-worker hours in the Bureau of Labor Statistics' monthly Employment Situation report or on electric power use by industry.

Capacity utilization is a measure of how close the nation's manufacturing sector is to running at full capacity. The Federal government defines full capacity as sustainable practical capacity, or the greatest level of output that a plant can maintain within the framework of a realistic work schedule, taking into account normal downtime and assuming sufficient availability or inputs to operate the machinery and equipment in place.

The report contains capacity and capacity utilization rates for 85 industries, including the following major categories:

- semiconductors and related electronic components
- motor vehicles and parts
- apparel and leather
- paper
- chemicals

- wood products
- electric utilities

Institute for Supply Management Indices

The Purchasing Managers' Index (PMI) garners quite a lot of attention, and it has been said that it was former Federal Reserve chairman Alan Greenspan's Desert Island Statistic—the one he would need to conduct policy if he were stranded on a desert island and only had access to one economic indicator. The PMI is the headline index of the Manufacturing ISM Report on Business. This report is created by the Tempe, Arizona based Institute for Supply Management (ISM), a non-profit professional association, and is made available on ISM's website at www.ism.ws on the first business day of every month, after 10 a.m. (EST).

The Report on Business discusses the current readings of ten seasonally adjusted diffusion indices constructed by the ISM from the responses to a survey of approximately 400 purchasing managers across the United States. The survey polls participants about their opinions on prices of materials paid in the production process, production levels, new orders, order backlog, the speed of supplier deliveries, inventories, customer inventories, employment, new export orders, and imports. The PMI is a weighted composite of the following five indices:

- new orders
- production
- employment
- vendor performance
- inventories

The ISM manufacturing report is valued not only for the diffusion indices but also for the accompanying discussion and comments made by the purchasing and supply executives participating in the survey. Together, the indices and executives' anecdotal insights form a fairly detailed picture of the state of the manufacturing sector.

Manufacturers' Shipments, Inventories, and Orders

The Manufacturers' Shipments, Inventories, and Orders, or M3 survey is one of the most respected economic indicators. Published monthly by the U.S. Department of Commerce's Census Bureau, the report measures current activity and future commitments in the U.S. manufacturing sector. Using data supplied by approximately 4,700 reporting units of businesses in 89 industry categories, it provides statistics on the value of factories' shipments, new orders, unfilled orders, and inventories.

The M3 survey is published in two parts. The Advance Report on Durable Goods is released about four weeks after the reference month, on approximately the eighteenth business day of the month. The revised and more comprehensive Manufacturers' Shipments, Inventories, and Orders appears about a week later and supplies greater detail about production, by industry group, as well as including information about nondurable and durable goods.

Manufacturing orders are considered to be a leading economic indicator because they reflect decisions about optimal inventory levels given the demand businesses anticipate based on their economic forecasts. The Census Bureau obtains its data on domestic manufacturing through surveys of manufacturing companies with annual shipments totaling $500 million or more. Participation is voluntary and responses are sent via the Internet, telephone or fax. The reports contain both seasonally adjusted and non-adjusted figures for the record month and for the previous three months, together with percentage changes from month-to-month. All the values are nominal, given in constant-dollar terms.

The M3 report is considered a gold mine of economic information. The durable new orders data is touted as a particularly rich lode due to the insight provided into a large component of personal consumption and capital expenditures. The M3 survey can be found on the Census Bureau's website at www.census.gov/indicator/www/M3/index.html.

Manufacturing and Trade Inventories and Sales

Business inventories are "waiting room" goods—products that have been manufactured, processed, or mined but have not yet been sold to the final user. As such, they are a key component of the GDP calculation. GDP is the total amount of final goods and services produced in an economy in a given period. That includes goods that haven't been acquired by a final purchaser, otherwise known as inventory.

However, inventories' role in the GDP calculation is not the sole reason economists monitor them carefully. Failure to balance inventories against demand can, and has, hurt businesses and destabilized the economy. Companies that overstock their shelves in anticipation of orders that do not materialize find themselves in a hole, forced to cut production and lay off workers. It has been hypothesized by prominent economists that the Great Crash of 1929 was provoked in part by the misalignment of inventory positions. On the other hand, businesses whose inventories are too lean may miss potential profit during a boom.

The MTIS report compiles sales data previously reported in the Census Bureau's Advance Monthly Sales for Retail Trade and Food Services report together with inventory and sales information from its Wholesale Trade Survey and its Manufacturers' Shipments, Inventories, and Orders survey.

Low inventory positions may signal an impending acceleration in production and manufacturing activity, while high inventories may portend a recession and widespread layoffs.

New Residential Construction

The American Dream of home ownership is one of the primary drivers of the U.S. economy. Housing activity affects the investment (I) component of the aggregate expenditure formula for calculating gross domestic product: C+I+G+(X-M). The construction of new, privately-owned residential structures, particularly single-family homes, is very telling regarding consumer sentiment and the health of the economy.

While new housing only accounts for three percent of GDP, it can have a profound effect on the economy due to the multiplier effect of related spending and other indirect contributions. Once a home is bought, it must be furnished and decorated. All of this activity means new jobs for construction workers, retail salespeople, and manufacturers, increased tax revenues for local and state municipalities, and greater spending on goods such as carpeting, furniture, and appliances.

There are several important housing indicators, including the Census Bureau's new home sales and the National Association of Realtors' existing home sales. The most influential, however, is new-housing starts and building permits. These numbers are contained in New Residential Construction, which is released jointly by the U.S. Department of Commerce's Census Bureau and the U.S. Department of Housing and Urban Development at 8:30 a.m. (EST) on approximately the fifteenth day of the month following the reference month. This release can be found on the Census Bureaus' website at www.census.gov/const/www/newresconstindex.html.

The Conference Board's Consumer Confidence and University of Michigan Consumer Sentiment Indices

Many different surveys of consumer confidence and sentiment exist. Some research institutions and investment firms have even created their own. The best known and most respected are the Conference Board's Consumer Confidence Index and the University of Michigan's

119

Index of Consumer Sentiment. However, all the various surveys share one characteristic: they ask everyday people from different walks of life easy to answer questions that probe their feelings about the current and future state of the economy, inflation, and their plans for vehicle and home purchases.

The Conference Board's confidence index is generally released on the last Tuesday of each month and a basic version made available on the Conference Board's website, www.conference-board.org. A more detailed version and the history are available by subscription directly from the Conference Board.

The University of Michigan usually issues its sentiment index on the second to last Friday of each month, followed by the revised final estimate two weeks later. This survey is available by subscription only.

The differences in the methodologies used by the Conference Board and the University of Michigan's Survey Research Center are small but important enough to produce indices with somewhat divergent characteristics and strengths. Some feel that the larger pool sampled in the NFO survey makes the Conference Board's indices more significant statistically. They also feel that eliciting expectations for the next six months, as the NFO survey does, is more realistic than the Michigan survey's five-year perspective. On the other hand, the longer history and twice-monthly reporting of the sentiment indices garner favor for the University of Michigan's report.

Advance Monthly Sales for Retail Trade and Food Services

The Census Bureau of the U.S. Department of Commerce releases the Advance Monthly Sales for Retail Trade and Food Services report, also known as the retail sales report, about two weeks after the end of the record month at 8:30 a.m. (EST). The report presents preliminary estimates for the nominal dollar value of sales for the retail sector, as well as the month-to-month change in that value. It is available on the Census Bureau's website at www.census.gov/svsd/www/fullpub.html.

The reason for the interest in the retail sales report is that retail spending provides a great deal of insight into personal consumption expenditures, the largest contributor to gross domestic product.

The Census Bureau compiles the Advance Monthly Sales for Retail Trade and Food Services report from responses to a survey it mails out to approximately 5,000 companies about five working days before the end of the reporting month. The 5,000 are a sub sample of the 13,000 or so companies polled for the later Monthly Retail Trade report. The replies are weighted and benchmarked to give an accurate representation of the more than three million retail and food services companies in the United States and indicates what these companies earned during the record month from sales and for providing services that are "incidental to the sale of the merchandise."

Personal Income and Outlays

The monthly Personal Income and Outlays report is produced by the Bureau of Economic Analysis and contains great detail on income-related measures as well as spending data for almost every imaginable good and service. The Personal Income and Outlays report is released about four weeks after the record month, on the first business day following the release of the Gross Domestic Product report at 8:30 a.m. (EST). It is available on the BEA's website at www.bea.gov.

The BEA uses the spending data in the report to compile the consumption expenditures portion of the GDP report. Consumer spending accounts for approximately 70 percent of all economic activity in the U.S. Strong spending is touted as a sign of an expansionary climate; slower spending signals softer economic conditions and income data is thought to provide insight into future spending and thus future economic activity.

The BEA calculates personal income by adding together income from seven major sources and then subtracting personal contributions for unemployment, disability, hospital, and old age survivors insurance. Then, by subtracting personal tax and nontax payments such as donations, fees, and fines, they arrive at disposable personal income. This is thought to be more useful than personal income because it represents the money that households have available to spend or to save.

Personal consumption expenditures are defined as the goods and services individuals buy, the operating expenses of non-profit institutions serving individuals, and the value of food, fuel, clothing, rentals, and financial services that individuals receive in kind.

Consumer and Producer Price Indices

When the price of goods and services rise, it is called inflation. Certain levels of inflation in the economy are considered normal and healthy. In contrast, accelerating inflation can cause severe problems, sometimes sparking recession. The Consumer Price Index (CPI) and the Producer Price Index (PPI) are touted as timely and detailed inflation indicators. The Bureau of Labor Statistics (BLS) calculates and reports on the CPI and the PPI. These reports are released around the middle of the month following the record month, and the PPI is usually at least one business day before the CPI. These reports are published at 8:30 a.m. (EST) and can be found on the BLS website, www.bls.gov.

The CPI tracks the change in price at the consumer level of a weighted basket of a few hundred goods and services. The PPI, also referred to as the wholesale price index, tracks changes in the selling prices of some 3,450 items at various stages of manufacture.

The PPI and CPI indices aren't generally considered leading indicators. Changes in the price levels do tell a great deal about the microeconomic conditions of individual commodities or industries; however, be careful not to read too much into a single month's activity.

Glossary

Actuals—The commodity itself.

Ascending triangle—A price pattern that occurs between a rising trend line at the bottom and a horizontal resistance line at the top. This pattern is generally considered bullish.

Ask—The ask price normally quoted is the lowest price at which anyone is willing to sell. Also known as an offer (vs. bid).

Base Currency—The currency in which an issuer or a trader maintains its book of accounts. In the FX market, the U.S. dollar is normally the base currency for quoting purposes. This means that quotes are expressed as a unit of $1 USD per the other currency quoted in the pair. The primary exceptions to this rule are the Australian dollar, the British pound, and the euro.

Basis Point—One graduation on a 100.00 point scale used in expressing variations in the yields on T-bills or Eurodollars

Bear (or bearish)—A belief that the market will decline; a market in which prices are declining.

Bid—Often referred to as a quotation or quote. It is an offer to buy at a specific price. The bid is the highest price anyone has declared that a trader wants to pay (vs. ask).

Break—A rapid and sharp decline in prices.

Breakout—A movement in the price out of an established trading range either above a resistance level or below a support level.

Broker—An agent who executes the buy and sell orders of a customer for a fee.

Bucketing—The unauthorized and illegal use of the customer's margin deposit. Also, it is accepting orders to buy and sell without executing these orders. Company's accused of this practice will commonly be referred to as Bucket Shops.

Bulge—A rapid increase in prices.

Bull (or bullish)—A belief that the market will rise; a market in which prices are rising.

Bundesbank—Germany's Central Bank.

Cable—The British pound; this term usually represents the currency pair GBP/USD.

Charting—The use of charts and graphs to assist in the analysis of market behavior, such as trends of price movements, average movements of price, and open interest.

Churning—Excessive trading in a customer's account. The term suggests that the representative ignores the objectives and interests of the client and seeks only to increase commissions.

Commingling—An illegal practice of mixing customer funds with funds of the commodity firm.

Commodity Futures Trading Commission (CFTC)—The independent federal agency established by the U.S. Congress under a major revision of the Commodity Exchange Act. The CFTC has an overall responsibility to regulate the futures industry in the United States.

Commodity Pool—An enterprise in which funds are contributed by a number of persons and combined in one account for the purpose of trading futures contracts and/or commodity options.

Commodity Pool Operator (CPO)—An individual or firm that operates or solicits funds for a commodity pool.

Commodity Trading Advisor (CTA)—An individual or firm who, for compensation or profit, directly or indirectly advises others as to the value of or the advisability of buying or selling. Providing advice indirectly includes exercising trading authority over a customer's account, as well as giving advice through written publications or other media.

Confirmation—Having more than one market factor agree with one another, for instance two indicators signaling bullish or bearish moves or an indicator and a chart pattern indicating the same bullish or bearish move.

Confirmation Statement—A written notification sent to a customer indicating that a trade has been executed and summarizing the details of the transaction. It must be sent no later than the business day following the execution.

Congestion—The sideways movement in the price; it represents trading in a narrow range.

Continuation pattern—Price patterns that indicate a consolidation in the prevailing trend, such as triangles, flags, and pennants.

Counterparty—One of the participants in a financial transaction

Day Trader—A speculator who takes positions and offsets those positions in the same trading session.

Descending Triangle—A price pattern that occurs between a falling trend line at the top and a horizontal support line at the bottom. This pattern is generally considered bearish.

Devaluation—A reduction in the exchange value of a currency.

Discretionary Account—An account in which the customer gives the broker or another party trading authority to buy and sell on his behalf, also called a managed account.

Divergence—Having more than one market factor disagree with each other. Divergences are usually seen as warnings of a trend reversal.

Ease off—A small, slow drop in the price.

Electronic Communication Network (ECN)—A system that brings together buyers and sellers. One of the downsides to these networks is that there is no guarantee that a trade will be executed, nor at a fair market price. Traders often must wait until the market opens the following day to receive a tighter spread.

Economic Indicator—A government-generated statistic that reflects current economic growth and stability of a country. Such indicators include employment rates, Gross Domestic Product (GDP), inflation, retail sales, etc.

Equity—The total cash value of an account, including the amount of profit or loss that would be incurred if the existing positions were liquidated at the current settlement price.

Euro—The single currency used by many European countries. It has replaced several currencies, such as the French franc and the Deutsche mark.

European Central Bank (ECB)—The Central Bank for the European Monetary Union.

Exchange Rate—The value of one currency in terms of another currency.

Federal Reserve (The Fed)—The Central Bank for the United States.

Fundamental Analysis—The examination of underlying factors of supply and demand in an attempt to determine market behavior.

Futures Commission Merchant (FCM)—An individual or firm that solicits or accepts orders to buy or sell futures contracts of commodity options and accepts money or other assets from customers to cover these costs.

Head and Shoulders—A technical trading pattern that resembles a head and two shoulders. The price reaches one plateau, the goes higher still, and then drops back to the plateau again. A top head and shoulders signifies the reversal of an upward trend. A bottom head and shoulder pattern signifies the reversal of a downward trend.

Hedging—The use of contracts to reduce price risk.

Initial Margin—The amount of money that is required to be deposited in an account when a futures position is established. Also called original margin.

Introducing Broker (IB)—An individual or firm that solicits or accepts orders to buy or sell futures contracts or commodity options but does not accept money or other assets from customers to cover the orders.

Intervention—An attempt by a central bank to intentionally move the exchange rate.

Leading Indicator—Statistics that are used to anticipate future economic activity.

Leverage—Using a range of financial instruments to increase the return of an investment

Limit Order—An order to buy or sell at a specified price or better. Also called a resting order.

Liquid Market—An actively traded market; a market that has a large number of active buyers and sellers.

Long Position—The purchase of a contract with the intention of selling at a future date.

Lot—Unit of trading in commodities; one contract of the commodity.

Maintenance Margin—The level to which the initial margin may decrease without the customer being called for additional margin.

127

Margin—A good faith deposit or performance bond whereby the customer deposits the required cash to indicate his willingness and ability to perform on the contract.

Margin Call—A request sent out by a firm to a customer when the margin in the account falls below the required maintenance margin level. The call requires that the customer restore the margin in the account back to the initial margin level.

Monthly Statements—A statement sent to a customer at the end of a statement period.

National Futures Association (NFA) – A self-regulatory futures industry association. Its regulatory powers are delegated by the CFTC. Its responsibility is to regulate members on how they conduct their business with the public.

Offer (Ask)—The proposal to sell at a given price (vs. Bid).

Omnibus Account – An account carried by a clearinghouse member Futures Commission Merchant for another non-clearing house member FCM in which the transactions are combined rather than designated separately and the identity of the individual accounts is not disclosed.

Open Position—A position that is not yet offset or liquidated.

Overbought—The determination that the price of a commodity has increased to an unreasonable level.

Oversold—The determination that the price of a commodity has declined to an unreasonable level.

Pip—The fourth decimal place to the right in the currency price (i.e., 0.0001).

Position Trader—A speculator who holds a position for more than one trading session.

Price Manipulation—An illegal practice used to cause or create prices that do not reflect natural price levels.

Range—The difference between the high and the low prices during a specified period of time.

Resistance—The upper bound of an established trading range where selling pressure tends to cause the price of futures to decline (vs. Support).

Retracement—A price movement in the opposite direction of the previous trend.

Risk Capital—Capital that is not needed for ordinary living expenses.

Round Turn—Commission charged by an FCM for both the purchase and subsequent sale of a contract, or the sale and subsequent purchase of a contract.

Scalper—A trader who day trades for his personal account many times in a single trading session in hopes of making a small profit on each trade.

Short—The sale of a contract with the intention of buying at a future date.

Speculator—A trader who buys and sells contracts for the purpose of making a profit. A speculator will buy contracts when he expects the price will rise and sell futures when he expects the price will fall.

Spot—Commodities available for immediate delivery for immediate payment. Also called Actual or Cash.

Spread—The simultaneous purchase of one contract against the sale of a related contract.

Sterling—The British pound.

Stop Order—An order to buy or sell at the market if the contract trades at or through a specified price. A stop order to sell becomes a market order if the contract trades at or below, or is offered at or below the stop price. A stop order to buy becomes a market order if the contract trades at or above, or is bid at or above the stop price.

Straddle—A strategy in which options to buy and sell the same security are purchased at the same time in order to avoid risk.

Support—The lower bound of an established trading range where buying pressure tends to cause the price to increase (vs. Resistance).

Swap—The trading of one security for another, especially when investment regulations have changed.

Swissy—The Swiss franc.

Technical Analysis—The analysis of past price data to determine future price movements.

Trend—The general direction of price movement, either upward or downward.

Volatility—A measure of a security's tendency to move up and down in price.

Whipsaw—Losing money on both sides of a swing trade.

Yard—A billion units of currency.

About the Author

Marilyn McDonald is an accomplished speaker, author, forex trader, and a series 3 licensed Futures Broker. As marketing director for InterbankFX, she manages their expansive InterbankFX University and conducts lectures on an international circuit. Marilyn has dedicated herself to preparing and educating traders for entrance into the forex market. Marilyn also publishes articles in all major trading publications. Some of these articles can be viewed at www.marilynmcdonald.net.

This book, along with other books, is available at discounts that make it realistic to provide it as a gift to your customers, clients, and staff. For more information on these long lasting, cost effective premiums, please call us at (800) 272-2855 or you may email us at sales@traderslibrary.com.